Contents

Foreword

The fabrication or induction of illness in children is a relatively rare form of child abuse. Where concerns exist about fabricated or induced illness, it requires professionals to work together, evaluating all the available evidence, in order to reach an understanding of the reasons for the child's signs and symptoms of illness. The management of these cases requires a careful medical evaluation which considers a range of possible diagnoses. At all times professionals need to keep an open mind to ensure that they have not missed a vital piece of information.

By their nature these types of cases require expert input from a range of disciplines, in particular paediatricians. It is, therefore, essential that all professionals who come into contact with children whose signs and symptoms may be being induced or fabricated are aware that this form of abuse exists and know what to do and who to speak to within their own organisation or a statutory one such as the police or local authority children's social care services.

Professionals working across health, social care, education, schools, the police and the independent sector should have an awareness of the possible ways in which illness can be induced or fabricated. Equally importantly, they should have an awareness of their respective roles and responsibilities and how they should work together from the point at which concerns are considered.

This guidance outlines what is known about fabricated or induced illness, the ways in which it can be caused, the impact on the child's health and development, and roles and functions of relevant agencies and procedures practitioners should follow where there are concerns about possible fabrication or induction of illness.

We hope that it will help professionals in the complex task of identifying those children in whom illness is being induced or fabricated and prevent them from suffering further harm. In addition we hope that both the children and families will be provided with the services which are necessary to enable these children to achieve the best possible outcomes.

KEVIN BRENNAN MP
Parliamentary Under Secretary of
State For Children, Young People
and Families

ANN KEEN MP
Parliamentary Under Secretary of
State For Health Services

VERNON COAKER MP
Parliamentary Under Secretary of
State For Crime Reduction

Chapter One
The scope and purpose of this document

Introduction

1.1 This document is based on *Working Together to Safeguard Children*: *A guide to inter-agency working to safeguard and promote the welfare of children* (HM Government 2006) and the *Framework for the Assessment of Children in Need and their Families* (Department of Health et al, 2000). *Working Together* sets out how all agencies and professionals should work together to safeguard and promote children's welfare. The Assessment Framework outlines a framework for use by all those who work with children and families determining whether a child is in need under the Children Act 1989 and deciding how best to provide help.

1.2 This supplementary guidance *Safeguarding Children in whom Illness is Fabricated or Induced* is intended to provide a national framework within which agencies and professionals at local level – individually and jointly – draw up and agree upon their own more detailed ways of working together where illness may be being fabricated or induced in a child by a carer who has parenting responsibilities for him or her. It is addressed to those who work in health, education, schools, probation and social care, the police and all others whose work brings them into contact with children and families. It is relevant to those working in the statutory, voluntary and independent sectors. **It is intended that Local Safeguarding Children Boards' (LSCBs) local safeguarding children procedures should incorporate this guidance and its references to Covert Video Surveillance, rather than having separate guidance on fabricated or induced illness in children. Within local procedures, the section on the use of covert video surveillance should make reference to the good practice advice for police officers which is available to them from the National Crime Faculty.**

1.3 The fabrication or induction of illness in children by a carer has been referred to by a number of different terms, most commonly Munchausen Syndrome by Proxy (Meadow, 1977), Factitious Illness by Proxy (Bools, 1996; Jones and Bools, 1999) or Illness Induction syndrome (Gray et al, 1995). This terminology is also used by some as if it were a psychiatric diagnosis.

1.4 The use of terminology to describe the fabrication or induction of illness in a child has been the subject of considerable debate between professionals. These differences in the use of terminology may result in a loss of focus on the welfare of the child. In order to keep the child's safety and welfare as the primary focus of all professional activity, this guidance refers to the '**fabrication or induction of illness in a child**' rather than using a particular term. If, as a result of a carer's behaviour, there is concern that the child is or is likely to suffer significant harm, this guidance should be followed. The key issue is not what term to use to describe this type of abuse, but the impact of fabricated or induced illness on the child's health and development, and consideration of how best to safeguard and promote the child's welfare.

1.5 There are three main ways of the carer fabricating or inducing illness in a child. These are not mutually exclusive and include:

- **fabrication** of signs and symptoms. This may include fabrication of past medical history;

- **fabrication** of signs and symptoms and **falsification** of hospital charts and records, and specimens of bodily fluids. This may also include falsification of letters and documents;

- **induction** of illness by a variety of means.

Examples of the types of abusive behaviours exhibited are further elaborated in paragraph 2.6, and paragraph 4.5 sets out the types of situations which may cause concern about a child's welfare.

1.6 In the guidance the term 'carer' is used to mean 'parent or carer', i.e. any adult who is exercising parenting responsibilities for a child. Those with parenting responsibilities may include, for example, grandparents, foster-parents, child minders, as well as those who have parental responsibility as defined in the Children Act 1989. **In situations where a staff member is suspected of causing harm to a child by inducing or fabricating illness, the procedures set out in paragraphs 6.20 – 6.30 in *Working Together* (2006).**

The status of this guidance

1.7 This guidance, issued by HM Government, is supplementary to *Working Together to Safeguard Children* (2006) and should be followed in conjunction with the main guidance. All assessments should be undertaken in accordance with the *Framework for the Assessment of Children in Need and their Families*. Where appropriate, paragraphs are cross-referenced to *Working Together* and the *Assessment Framework*.

1.8 **The guidance is issued under Section 7 of the Local Authority Social Services Act 1970, which requires local authorities in their social services functions to act under the general guidance of the Secretary of State. It should be complied with by LAs carrying out their social services functions unless local circumstances indicate exceptional reasons that justify a variation. It is also issued under s16 of the Children Act 2004 which states that Children's Services Authorities and each of their Board partners, in exercising their functions in relation to LSCBs, must have regard to any guidance given to them by the Secretary of State for that purpose.**

1.9 Where this document is not statutory guidance for a particular organisation, it still represents a standard of good practice and will help organisations fulfil their duties in co-operation with partners. For example, managers and staff with particular responsibilities in the organisations covered by the duty to safeguard and promote the welfare of children in section 11 of the Children Act 2004 (found at: www.everychildmatters.gov.uk/socialcare/safeguarding/) are encouraged to read this document and follow it in conjunction with the section 11 guidance (HM Government, 2007). The same principle applies to educational institutions with duties under sections 157 & 175 of the Education Act 2002 regarding safeguarding and promoting the welfare of children.

The role of this guidance

1.10 Processes and procedures are never ends in themselves, but should always be used as a means of bringing about better outcomes for children. No guidance can, or should attempt to, offer a detailed prescription for working with each child and family. Work with children and families where there are concerns about a child's welfare, is sensitive and difficult. Work in situations where illness has been fabricated or induced can be very stressful. Good practice calls for effective co-operation between different agencies and professionals; sensitive work with parents and carers in the best interests of the child; and the careful exercise of professional judgement, based on thorough assessment and critical analysis of the available information.

1.11 The Royal College of Paediatrics and Child Health published a report on *Fabricated or Induced Illness by Carers* (2002). It describes the role of paediatricians and other child healthcare professionals and recommends how they should work with professionals from other agencies. The Royal College's report informed the development of this guidance and provides more in-depth information for professionals, particularly those in health. The College's report is currently being updated to take account of *Working Together* (2006) and recent clinical developments.

1.12 In 2000 the *Report of a review of the research framework in North Staffordshire Hospital NHS Trust* (Department of Health, 2000b) was published. It called for a wide range of measures to improve research governance across the NHS. In addition, it recommended the development of guidelines to assist the identification of children who have had illnesses fabricated or induced by their carer. The Department of Health responded to this later recommendation with a commitment to produce "new guidelines for professional practice and interagency working in responding to concerns that a child may be having illness feigned or induced by a carer. These guidelines will be drawn up within the framework of *Working Together to Safeguard Children: A guide to inter-agency working to safeguard and promote the welfare of children* (1999)". The first edition of the guidance, issued in 2002, has now been updated following the publication of the revised *Working Together to Safeguard Children* (2006).

1.13 **This guidance suggests that where there is any potential for the use of covert video surveillance the police should be informed and, within the multi-agency team, take the lead in co-ordinating such action** (see paragraphs 6.35 – 6.40). All action should be undertaken in accordance with the LSCB safeguarding children procedures. Legal advice should be taken where there is any doubt about the use of covert video surveillance.

An integrated approach

1.14 Children have varying needs which change over time. Judgements on how best to intervene when there are concerns about harm to a child will often and unavoidably entail an element of risk – the two extremes being leaving a child for too long in a dangerous situation or removing a child unnecessarily from their family. The way to proceed in the face of uncertainty is through competent professional judgements based on a sound assessment of the child's needs, the parents' capacity to respond to those needs – including their capacity to keep the child safe from significant harm – and the wider family circumstances (*Working Together*, 2006).

1.15 Effective measures to safeguard children cannot be seen in isolation from the wider range of support and services available to meet the needs of children and families:

- many of the families in which a child has had illness fabricated or induced have experienced a number of stress factors in their lives. Providing services and support to these children and families may strengthen the capacity of parents to respond to the needs of these children before they reach the point where their reaction to their difficulties is to fabricate or induce illness in their child;

- enquiries under s47 of the Children Act 1989 may reveal significant unmet needs for support and services among children and families, particularly in relation to the needs of the parents and the way in which the family members relate to each other. These should always be explicitly addressed if the family member so wishes, even where concerns are not substantiated about significant harm to a child;

- if safeguarding children processes are to result in improved outcomes for children, then effective plans for safeguarding and promoting each child's welfare should be based on a wide ranging assessment of the needs of the child and their family circumstances, taking account of past histories of all family members;

- all work with children and families should retain a clear focus on the welfare of the child. Just as safeguarding children processes should always consider the wider needs of the child and family, so broad-based family support services should always be alert to, and know how to respond quickly and decisively to potential indicators of illness being fabricated or induced in a child.

A shared responsibility

1.16 Safeguarding and promoting the welfare of children depends crucially upon effective information sharing, collaboration and understanding between agencies and professionals. These relationships may become strained where there are concerns that illness is being fabricated or induced in a child and there are differences in opinion about how best to safeguard the child's welfare or indeed if the child is being abused. Constructive relationships between individual workers should be supported by a strong lead from elected or appointed authority members, and the commitment of senior officers from each agency.

1.17 At the strategic level, agencies and professionals should cooperate with each other and involve service users, to plan comprehensive and co-ordinated children's services which have the capacity to respond to the identified needs of children. Children who have had illness fabricated or induced and their families are likely to require specialised services, some of which may not be available locally and will have to be secured from either regional or national resources. One case can make considerable demands on an agency's available resources. On these rare occasions, senior managers should be involved in deciding how to allocate resources deemed necessary to bring about the best outcomes for the child.

1.18 Children who have had illness fabricated or induced are likely to require co-ordinated help from a range of agencies such as health, social care (adults' and children's), education, schools and the voluntary and independent sectors over a sustained period of time. The nature of this input is likely to change as the child develops and his or her needs change; over time, therefore, the types of services required may differ considerably.

1.19 For those children who are suffering, or at risk of suffering significant harm, joint working is essential, to safeguard the welfare of children and – where necessary – to take action, within the criminal justice system, regarding the perpetrators of crimes against children. In using this guidance all agencies and professionals should:

- be alert to potential indicators of illness being fabricated or induced in a child;

- be alert to the risk of harm which individual abusers, or potential abusers, may pose to children in whom illness is being fabricated or induced;

- share, and help to analyse information so that an informed assessment can be made of the child's needs and circumstances;

- contribute to whatever actions (including the cessation of unnecessary medical tests and treatments) and services are required to safeguard and promote the child's welfare and

  - regularly review the outcomes for the child against specific planned outcomes

  - work co-operatively with parents unless to do so would place the child at increased risk of harm;

- assist in providing relevant evidence in any criminal or civil proceedings, should this course of action be deemed necessary.

Chapter Two
Some lessons from research
and experience

Introduction

2.1 Our knowledge and understanding of children's welfare – and how to respond in the best interests of a child to concerns about abuse and neglect – develop over time, informed by research, experience, and the critical scrutiny of practice. Sound professional practice involves making judgements, supported by evidence derived from research and experience, about the nature and impact of abuse and neglect, and when and how to intervene to improve outcomes for children; and information derived from a thorough assessment of a specific child's health, development and welfare, parental capacity and his or her family circumstances.

2.2 This chapter begins by reporting research findings on the incidence and prevalence of illness being fabricated or induced in a child by a carer and describes some of the types of behaviours exhibited by carers which can be associated with illness fabrication or induction. It goes on to summarise available research findings and practice experience specific to this type of abuse, and concludes with what is known about how best to secure optimal outcomes for children in whom illness has been fabricated or induced.

Incidence and prevalence

2.3 The fabrication or induction of illness in a child by a carer has been considered to be rare (however, see below). McClure at al (1996) carried out a two-year study to determine the epidemiology of Munchausen Syndrome by Proxy, non-accidental poisoning and non-accidental suffocation in the UK and the Republic of Ireland. They analysed data from 128 confirmed cases notified to the British Paediatric Association Surveillance Unit during the period September 1992 to August 1994. Based on this data, the researchers estimated that the combined annual incidence in the British Isles of these forms of abuse in children under 16 years was at least 0.5 per 100,000 and for children under 1 years at least 2.8 per 100,000. The authors calculated that "in a hypothetical district of one million inhabitants therefore, the expected incidence would be approximately one child per year" (p. 58).

2.4 This study showed that reported rates of fabricated or induced illness varied greatly between different health service regions and the researchers suggested it was under-reported nationally. At the time of their study their findings also suggested that paediatricians considered that the identification had to be virtually certain before a child protection conference is initiated. Thus a number of cases may be unrecorded because of the absence of irrefutable evidence in situations where the level of concern about harm to the child is extremely high. The cases may also present in ways which result in unnecessary medical interventions, for example, where symptoms are verbally reported to surgeons who then carry out operations without questioning the basis of this information. Consequently the estimate of one child per one million head of population is likely to be an under-estimate.

Carers' behaviours associated with fabricated or induced illness

2.5 Carers exhibit a range of behaviours when they wish to convince others that their child is ill. A key professional task is to distinguish between the very anxious carer who may be responding in a reasonable way to a very sick child and those who exhibit abnormal behaviour (see paragraphs 4.1 – 4.3). Such abnormal behaviour in a carer can be present in one or both carers and often involves passive compliance of the child (see paragraph 2.22). These carer behaviours may constitute ill treatment (section 31(9) of the Children Act 1989).

2.6 The following list is of behaviours exhibited by carers which can be associated with fabricating or inducing illness in a child. This list is not exhaustive and should be interpreted with an awareness of cultural behaviours and practices which can be mistakenly construed as abnormal behaviours:

- deliberately inducing symptoms in children by administering medication or other substances, by means of intentional transient airways obstruction or by interfering with the child's body so as to cause physical signs.

- interfering with treatments by over dosing with medication, not administering them or interfering with medical equipment such as infusion lines;

- claiming the child has symptoms which are unverifiable unless observed directly, such as pain, frequency of passing urine, vomiting or fits. These claims result in unnecessary investigations and treatments which may cause secondary physical problems;

- exaggerating symptoms which are unverifiable unless observed directly, causing professionals to undertake investigations and treatments which may be invasive, are unnecessary and therefore are harmful and possibly dangerous;

- obtaining specialist treatments or equipment for children who do not require them;

- alleging psychological illness in a child.

2.7 When a child is in hospital, it is usual for carers (usually the child's parents) to be very involved in the care of their child, including participating in medical tests, taking temperatures and measuring bodily outputs. Where illness is being fabricated or induced by a carer, these normal hospital practices afford the carer the opportunity to continue this behaviour. This may mean, for example, that treatments and tests may be interfered with and the reported signs and symptoms continue whilst the child is in hospital. Differences may be observed between the ways in which carers who fabricate or induce illness interact with their children compared with other carers.

Commonly, these carers are observed to be intensely involved with their children, never taking a much needed break nor allowing anyone else (either family members or professionals) to undertake any of their child's care. This behaviour may preclude adequate observation of the child. Some, however, spend little time interacting with their child. They may be very involved with other families on the ward and hospital staff rather than with their child. Another observed feature is that some carers appear unusually unconcerned about the results of investigations which may be indicative of a serious physical illness in the child.

Responding to reported signs and symptoms

2.8 The majority of cases of fabricated or induced illness in children are confirmed in a hospital setting because either medical findings or their absence provide evidence of this type of abuse.

Early history and concern about the child's health

2.9 A significant number of children in whom illness is fabricated or induced will have been well known to health professionals from birth. Some also suffer from a verified acute or chronic medical condition. Some may previously have been seriously ill, for example as a consequence of prematurity, while others may have had minor problems at birth or in their first few months of life. Consideration should be given to the possibility that the obstetric complications themselves may have been due to the mother interfering with her pregnancy to induce a premature birth (Jureidini, 1993). Children may have also experienced other forms of abuse, for example, physical abuse or neglect, prior to the identification of fabricated or induced illness (Bools et al, 1992).

2.10 Children in this group often present with, or have a past history of both genuine and perceived feeding difficulties, faltering growth and reported allergies (Bools et al, 1992; Gray and Bentovim, 1996; Rosenberg, 1987).

2.11 At the point that fabrication or induction of illness is confirmed the child may have organic problems which will require ongoing medical treatment. These may pre-date the abuse or be a consequence of it. It can be difficult to identify retrospectively the origins of a child's medical problems but, following identification of fabricated or induced illness, treatment for medical conditions should be undertaken as part of the child's overall plan.

2.12 The medical histories of this group of children are likely to have started early and in many instances will have become extensive by the time the suspected abuse is identified. Some children may have been referred to a tertiary paediatric centre because they were thought to have a serious or rare illness requiring expert diagnosis and treatment. They may have been seen at many hospitals in different geographical areas and by a number of professionals. They may also have been seen in centres for alternative medicine or by private practitioners.

Impact of fabricated or induced illness on the child

Child death and morbidity

2.13 International research findings suggest that up to 10% of these children die and about 50% experience long-term consequent morbidity. In the British Isles study referred to in paragraph 2.3, McClure et al (1996) found that 8 out of 128 (6%) children died as a direct result of abuse. A further 15 (12%) required intensive care and an additional 45 (35%) suffered major physical illness, again as a result of abuse. The way in which a child's circumstances are managed will impact on their outcomes but the lives of some who present at hospital in a life-threatening situation, for example having been poisoned, might not be able to be saved.

2.14 In the McClure et al (1996) study, 83 (65%) of the 128 index children had at least one sibling and of these, 15 (12%) had a sibling who died previously (a total of 18 deaths). Five (4%) of these deaths had been classified as Sudden Infant Deaths. Information about a death or previous abuse of siblings may become known to professionals only after a family history has been collated. At the time of death some may have been unexplained or ascribed to natural causes, while others may have been known to have occurred as a result of abuse. Previous reported physical abuse of siblings is common in this group of children and previous abuse may have included the fabrication or induction of illness. A child may be considered to be at risk of significant harm because of abuse inflicted on siblings, or the death of siblings due to abuse.

Impact on the child's health and development

2.15 Many of the children who do not die as a result of having illness fabricated or induced suffer significant long-term consequences. These may include long-term impairment of their physical, psychological and emotional development (see paragraph 3.90 of Assessing Children in Need: Practice Guidance (Department of Health, 2000a)).

2.16 Fabrication of illness may not necessarily result in the child experiencing physical harm. Where children have not suffered physical harm, there may still be concern about them suffering emotional harm. Concerns about children being brought up in a fabricated sick role are further discussed in paragraph 2.21. Children may also suffer emotional harm as a result of an abnormal relationship with their mother (if she is responsible for the abuse) and their disturbed family relationships (see paragraphs 2.30 and 2.31).

2.17 In their follow-up study of 54 children who were known to have had illness induced or fabricated or induced, Bools et al (1993) found a range of emotional and behavioural disorders, and school related problems including difficulties in attention and concentration and non-attendance. These difficulties were present both in children who were living with their abusing parent and those who had been placed with alternative carers, suggesting the need for treatment regimes which specifically address the child's ongoing needs throughout childhood. McGuire and Feldman (1989) also reported a range of disorders in children known to have had illness fabricated or induced, depending on the age of the child; feeding disorders in infants, withdrawal and hyperactivity in pre-school children and direct fabrication or exaggeration of their own physical symptoms by older children and adolescents.

2.18 Whilst it is well documented that children who have been abused or neglected are likely to suffer impairment to their health and development, it cannot be assumed that all children suffering impairment have been abused. Where there are concerns about the reasons for a child's developmental delay, it is important to clarify the contributing factors and identify any underlying conditions. For some children the origins of their impairment or disability may be very complex with an underlying medical or developmental condition being further impaired by abuse or neglect. In these circumstances, detailed assessments are required to understand cause and effect (For further discussion, see Chapter 4: The Spectrum of Signs and Symptoms, Royal College of Child Health and Paediatrics, 2002).

The experience of the abused child

2.19 Where illness is being fabricated or induced, extensive, unnecessary medical investigations may be carried out in order to establish the underlying causes for the reported signs and symptoms. The child may also have treatments prescribed or operations which are unnecessary. These investigations can result in children spending long periods of time in hospital and some, by their nature, may also place the child at risk of suffering harm or even death.

2.20 Nearly all affected children undergo many unpleasant investigations and/or treatments but many children, especially young children, who have had illness fabricated or induced may not be fully aware of the nature of their abuse. Few studies have sought children's views on this matter, but Neale et al (1991), through their interviews with children, found that many had not been able to disclose the nature of their abuse, in part because of the skill of their mothers (the perpetrators) in teaching the children to present a rosy picture to the external world whilst they were being subjected to extensive physical and emotional abuse at home. Even after disclosure of the abuse and placement with alternative carers, some still wanted continued contact with them.

2.21 Some children are confused about their state of health. Many are preoccupied with anxieties about their health and survival and may express suicidal thoughts as a result of their despair. Older children and adults who have been abused in this way may come to feel anger at their betrayal by their parent(s), and a lack of trust in those caring for them including medical professionals.

Involvement by the child

2.22 In children who have had illness fabricated or induced, there seems to be a continuum of involvement with their carer, from naivety through to passive acceptance, actual participation and active self-harm (Sanders, 1995). Some children, particularly those who are older, may learn to collude with their carer in the management of a non-existent condition before eventually fabricating or inducing illness in themselves or developing a somatisation disorder. Such children can continue to be dependent on their carer and use her/him as a reference point for their own state of health. As a consequence of this dependency, some may lose the ability in childhood to identify true illness and become unable to act appropriately if they are ill. Some older children and adults feel guilty for their perceived collusion. So, just as with other forms of child abuse, the effects of illness having been fabricated or induced may impact on a child for life.

Age range of children

2.23 The age range of children in whom illness is fabricated or induced extends throughout childhood, although it is most commonly identified in younger children. In the McClure et al (1996) study, 77% of children were aged under 5 years at the time of identification with a median age of 20 months.

Age at onset of fabrication or induction

2.24 The age of the child when the fabrication or induction begins is usually much younger than when the abuse is identified because of the length of time it normally takes to identify this type of abuse. Schreier and Libow (1993), in their survey of 362 cases, found that the average length of time to identification was greater than 6 months in a third of the cases and more than a year in a fifth of the cases. Experience indicates that the duration may be of several years.

Gender of carer responsible for the abuse

2.25 Clinical evidence indicates that fabricated or induced illness is usually carried out by a female carer, usually the child's mother. Fathers and women other than the mothers have also been known to be responsible (Makar and Squier, 1990; Samuels et al, 1992). It is common in these latter cases for the adult to have undertaken significant responsibility for providing much of the child's daily care.

2.26 Therapeutic work undertaken with families has revealed the extent to which both mothers and fathers were involved in perpetuating the belief that the child was seriously ill. It is not, therefore, appropriate to always consider the fathers to be mere bystanders in the process of illness induction: their role in each particular family system must be understood as part of the assessment process (Griffith, 1988; Manthei et al, 1988).

Carers' previous histories

2.27 There is no evidence to support a unique profile of carers who fabricate or induce illness in their children. There is, however, evidence that as with many parents who abuse or neglect their children, specific aspects of their histories are likely to have been troubled. A careful assessment is required to understand the contribution which their past experiences have made to the child's illness fabrication or induction and the impact that past events may be having on their current ability to care for their child.

2.28 The child's carers, who are usually their parents, may have histories of having experienced childhood abuse or privation. This can include all forms of abuse, including emotional (Bools et al, 1994; Samuels et al, 1992).

2.29 The parents may also have considerable medical and psychiatric histories which may or may not be able to be verified independently. The same may be so in relation to the obstetric history of the mother. This information may not be easily accessible and considerable effort may be required to gather it together into a detailed chronology.

2.30 Reported features of the parent's health histories include:

- **Physical health**. A significant number of parents are likely to report having experienced genuine medical problems. They may or may not have been substantiated by medical investigations. They may also have a history of inflicting deliberate self-harm. The mothers may have a complicated obstetric history. For some mothers, there may have been professional concern about them causing their own miscarriages.

- **Psychiatric history**. A significant number of parents will have been assessed or treated for mental health problems. Following a formal psychiatric assessment, some may have been diagnosed with a personality disorder, but others may have no diagnosable psychiatric disorder (Bass and Adshead, 2007). **Paragraphs 3.52 – 3.63 on Adult Mental Health explore this area in more depth.**

2.31 Parents also report having suffered a number of significant bereavements or losses in their lives with these often having taken place within a relatively short time span (Gray and Bentovim, 1996). The bereavements may be of significant adults in their lives (a parent or other supportive family member), of offspring by miscarriage, stillbirth or child death and the losses of partners through divorce or separation.

Family relationships

2.32 Relationship problems between the child's parents are common, although they may not have been acknowledged prior to child welfare concerns being raised. Similarly, a number of parents may have experienced problems associated with taking on the role of parenthood. These may have been presented early on in their parenting careers.

2.33 In families where it has been identified that a child's illness has been fabricated or induced, these past problems are often revealed in the course of an assessment or therapeutic work. This knowledge may, however, not have been held by those professionals who had responsibility for the child's health care.

Long-term outcome for carers who fabricate or induce illness

2.34 There is no systematic research information available on the long-term outcomes for those carers who have received therapeutic help following identification of them fabricating or inducing illness in children (Bluglass, 2001; Brooke and Adshead, 2001). Some information is available from individual case studies (Nicol and Eccles, 1985; Black and Hollis, 1996; Coombe, 1995) and indirectly from research on outcomes for children. This means that decisions about the child's safety have to be made on a case by case basis drawing on professionals' knowledge base about the abuse or neglect of children.

Outcomes for children

2.35   There has been little research done on the longer-term outcomes for children in these circumstances, but the available evidence suggests that outcomes have been poor for many children who had illness fabricated or induced. In one such study, a cohort of 54 children who had experienced attempted suffocation, poisoning or having symptoms such as seizures fabricated was followed up on average 5.6 years after the abuse had been identified (Bools et al, 1993). Thirty of the children were living with their mother – the abuser – and 24 were in alternative care, either with family members or foster carers. Among the 30 children living with the original abuser, a third had had further illness fabricated and there were significant other types of concerns about another third. Many children placed in new families also suffered from psychological disorders, in many cases a continuation of an earlier disorder. The difficulties of 5 children where suffocation had been attempted were clearly related to their previous abusive experiences. Nearly half of the children had unacceptable outcomes including conduct and emotional disorders, and difficulties at school including non-attendance, in addition to re-abuse. An analysis of the findings from this study indicated that where at follow-up the children were being cared for by their mothers (who had been responsible for the abuse), a greater proportion of those who had an acceptable outcome had experienced a period in foster-care following identification of the abuse, compared with those who remained continuously with their mother.

2.36   In Davis' follow up study (median of 2 years) of children reported to have had an illness induced, none of their signs and symptoms had been found subsequently to be due to intrinsic organic disease (Davis et al, 1998). At follow-up, forty percent of the children were living at home with the abusing parent, but only 24% of those where they had been poisoned and only 10% of those where suffocation had been intentionally attempted. Thirty-three percent of the children still had their names on child protection register and 24% still had signs and symptoms due to fabricated or induced illness. Seventeen percent of those who had not suffered direct physical harm had nevertheless subsequently suffered further abuse.

2.37   The Park Hospital group (Berg and Jones, 1999) has reported the outcome of work with a consecutive series of 17 children and their families who were admitted to its inpatient family unit after the abuse had been identified. In 13 of the 17 cases selected on the basis of the likelihood of successful intervention, therapeutic work was undertaken to establish whether the child could be re-united with their family. Of these, it was recommended that 10 children should be reunited with their natural parents and 3 should be placed in alternative care as it was not considered sufficiently safe for them to return home. All these recommendations were followed and at an average of 27 months after discharge from the unit, the children had done well overall in terms of their development, growth and adjustment. One child, who had been re-abused by her mother, was subsequently being cared for solely by her father. From this follow-up study it has been "cautiously concluded that family re-unification is reasonable to attempt for a selected subgroup of cases of factitious illness by proxy but, where this is attempted, long-term follow-up is necessary in order to assure that psychological maltreatment does not occur and that the parent's mental health is monitored" (Berg and Jones, 1999).

2.38 Another study found that there was evidence of good outcomes for children where the child's safety had been addressed and long-term therapeutic work had been undertaken with families. This work was based on the findings of an assessment which identified the changes required in the family system for the child to be safe and achieve his or her optimal health and developmental milestones (Gray et al, 1995). These good outcomes occurred where cases were managed within a child protection framework, therapeutic interventions were focused on the protection of the child, a thorough assessment was undertaken of the family's functioning and its ability to change and protect the child, and clear decisions were made about whether the child was able to live with both parents, the non-abusing parent or should be placed in an alternative family context.

2.39 **In summary, following identification of fabricated or induced illness in a child by a carer, the way in which the case is managed will have a major impact on the developmental outcomes for the child. The extent to which the parents have acknowledged some responsibility for fabricating or inducing illness in their child will also affect these outcomes for the child.**

Chapter Three
Roles and responsibilities

Introduction

3.1 A clear understanding of the roles and responsibilities of organisations and practitioners is essential for effective collaboration. These are set out in Chapter 2 of *Working Together* (2006). This chapter outlines the main roles and responsibilities of statutory agencies, professionals, the voluntary and independent sectors, and the wider community in relation to circumstances where illness has been fabricated or induced in a child by a carer. Joint working should extend across the planning, management, provision and delivery of services. This chapter does not stand alone and, in particular, should be read in conjunction with Chapters 1 and 4 of this document.

Health

3.2 This section is divided into the roles and responsibilities of health organisations, health professionals and different health services.

Health organisations

Strategic Health Authorities (SHAs)

3.3 SHAs membership of LSCBs will enable them to satisfy themselves that local arrangements provide support for local health professionals in dealing with this sensitive and difficult area of work, and that local health service arrangements are in place to respond appropriately to all cases or suspected cases of fabricated and induced illness.

Primary Care Trusts

3.4 *Working Together* states that PCTs should identify a senior lead for children and young people to ensure their needs are at the forefront of local planning and service delivery. In addition, the named public health professional with responsibility for safeguarding children within the PCT should be familiar with the modes of presentation of fabricated or induced illness in a child and the extreme difficulties such cases may present, together with the need for senior practitioner involvement.

3.5   Support should be made available:

- for advice via the designated and named doctors and nurses in managing such cases;

- if covert video surveillance is to be used e.g. for funding of additional support staff and suitable rooms;

- for the staff involved, including ensuring their protection and ongoing support if necessary (the impact of identifying and working with such cases can be extremely stressful);

- in the preparation of any appropriate media handling strategy (which should be undertaken in conjunction with other agencies involved).

3.6   The PCT should ensure that appropriate training on fabricated or induced illness is made available to professional healthcare staff at all levels in all disciplines. The designated doctors and nurses should advise on the commissioning of this training, recognising that in any one year the average PCT is not likely to see many cases of fabricated or induced illness. PCTs should ensure that agencies with whom they have commissioning arrangements provide such training for their staff, and have systems and policies in place to respond to cases of fabricated or induced illness. They should also have a policy for resolving differences where there is disagreement between health professionals over identification, diagnosis or management decisions.

NHS Trusts and NHS Foundation Trusts, including Ambulance Trusts

3.7   Children with suspected fabricated or induced illness may present to the full range of medical specialists. This is most likely to be a general paediatrician or paediatricians providing specialist care, but may also include general, orthopaedic and paediatric surgeons, surgical specialities particularly ENT, ophthalmology, orthopaedics, gynaecology and dermatology. Concerns may be raised by services to whom the children present including pharmacists and allied health professionals. In addition, carers of children may be in receipt of adult services, and the professionals involved in their care may have concerns about the welfare of these children. This could include professionals providing obstetric and gynaecological care to women, mental health services and the full range of medical and surgical specialities. It is important that any concerns about the children's welfare are not conveyed to the carers until further assessment and multidisciplinary decisions have been made about how and by whom these will be discussed with both the child's parents. Every Trust should have a named doctor and nurse/midwife or professional in the case of ambulance trusts, with whom professional staff should liaise if they have concerns about a child's welfare.

3.8   In a very small number of cases, the use of covert video surveillance may be suggested. Decisions about its use should take place at a strategy discussion between relevant agencies and in particular, the police, children's social care, the consultant paediatrician responsible for the child's health care and the senior ward nurse. Senior officers of the relevant NHS Trusts should also be involved. **The Chief Executive of NHS Trust should be kept informed of any decisions to apply to use covert video surveillance in his/her Trust (see paragraphs 1.2 and 6.35 – 6.40 on covert video surveillance).**

3.9 Where it has been decided (at a strategy discussion) to carry out covert video surveillance because of the nature of concerns about how the child is suffering or likely to suffer significant harm, the police should undertake this action.

Health professionals

3.10 All health professionals in the NHS or private sector may come across illness being fabricated or induced in a child. Personnel in these services are well-placed to note the number of presentations of a child, and the manner and circumstances in which these children present. It is essential that health professionals, whether working with children or adults, should familiarise themselves with the various presentations of this type of child abuse. Health professionals may also identify a carer who is fabricating or inducing illness in themselves. In these circumstances, they should consider whether any child(ren) of this adult is/are having their health or development impaired.

3.11 All health personnel should be familiar with their LSCB safeguarding children procedures and, in particular, know who to contact when they have child welfare concerns. (Please see Chapter 4 in this guidance.) Close multi-disciplinary and inter-agency working is essential in these cases (Royal College of Paediatrics and Child Health, 2002).

3.12 Once a health practitioner has suspicions that fabricated or induced illness is being presented, he or she should consult the clinical manager (who has lead responsibility for contacting children's social care or the police) and/or the named or designated doctor or nurse for safeguarding children. The named doctor or nurse should be contacted for support and advice, but if unavailable, the designated doctor/nurse should be contacted. All health professionals should keep detailed notes of these discussions.

3.13 Health practitioners should not normally discuss their concerns with the parents/carers at this stage.

3.14 LSCB safeguarding children procedures should be followed. Children's social care should be informed of these concerns at the earliest possible opportunity. It has lead responsibility for undertaking an initial assessment and, if appropriate, should convene a strategy discussion. This discussion will determine subsequent actions which should be strictly adhered to and regularly reviewed.

3.15 Where there are suspicions of parents fabricating or inducing illness and the child is in hospital it is important to secure appropriately and to date relevant equipment e.g. syringes, feeding equipment and food/drink samples etc. for police investigation.

3.16 For all children, it is essential that careful and complete notes are kept at every stage, together with the reasons why decisions are taken, for example, not to inform the parents of concerns during particular periods in time in order to prevent the child suffering harm (see paragraphs 6.24 – 6.34 on record keeping).

3.17 If a child protection conference is convened information should be shared and discussed in order to inform decision making about how best to promote and safeguard the child's welfare.

Designated and named health professionals

3.18 Each PCT is responsible for ensuring it has a designated doctor and designated nurse to undertake the role of designated professionals for safeguarding children across the health economy. Further details about the role can be found in Chapter 2 of *Working Together*. These professionals are key to providing advice and support to named professionals and for staff dealing with cases of fabricated or induced illness, or suspected cases, as well as promoting, influencing and developing training on this issue.

3.19 All NHS Trusts, NHS Foundation Trusts and PCTs providing services for children should identify a named doctor and a named nurse / midwife for safeguarding. In the case of NHS Direct, Ambulance Trusts and independent providers, this should be a named professional. Further details about the role can be found in Chapter 2 of *Working Together*. These professionals are a source of advice and support for staff dealing with cases of fabricated or induced illness, or suspected cases, within their own organisation.

Paediatricians

3.20 At some time, all consultant paediatricians are likely to be faced with a child whom they suspect some or all of their signs and symptoms of illness are being fabricated or induced by a carer. This may include children referred to them or children with whom they are already involved. Whenever such concerns arise, the consultant responsible for the child's health care (i.e the responsible paediatric consultant) should take lead responsibility for all decisions about the child's health care – these should **not** be delegated to a more junior member of staff although they may be involved in the process of assessment and subsequent management under the consultant's supervision. This lead responsibility should include getting information from any relevant GPs or consultants who have treated the child. Where there are concerns about a child's safety and welfare, discussion with children's social care can be on the basis of suspicion of significant harm – it does not have to be proved before contacting children's social care. Referrals can also be made because the child is considered to be a child in need under section 17 of the Children Act 1989.

3.21 The responsible paediatric consultant should consult the named doctor about safeguarding concerns and keep him or her informed in the process. If the consultant is themselves the named doctor, they are advised to consult with the designated doctor. **Discussions with a senior colleague in children's social care may also be helpful in deciding whether and when a referral should be made.**

3.22 The Royal College of Paediatrics and Child Health Report on *Fabricated or Induced Illness by Carers* (2002) provides specific advice for paediatricians and other health professionals. In particular,

Chapter 5, *Medical Evaluation: Procedures and Management* should be followed in conjunction with this guidance when there are concerns about fabricated or induced illness in a child.

3.23 The responsible paediatric consultant should ensure a high standard of record keeping (paragraphs 6.24 – 6.34) and ensure the records are kept secure at all times .

3.24 In any case of suspected fabricated or induced illness it is essential to carefully review the child's medical history (see paragraph 6.21 on health professionals sharing information with each other). This should include reviewing all available medical notes and liaising with the child and family members' GP(s) and health visitor(s) or school nurse. If there are separate child health records these should be accessed and consideration given to making enquiries of other local hospitals (it is not unknown, particularly in an urban area, for a child to be under the care of more than one hospital). Likewise, if the family has recently moved, contact should be made with the paediatric and emergency care services in the previous area. The named doctor for the Trust from which notes are being sought can often facilitate this process. The drawing up of a detailed medical chronology is most important and will often confirm whether or not concerns of possible fabricated or induced illness require further evaluation and the urgency with which these should be undertaken. It can also help identify undiagnosed medical conditions. The organisations named health professionals for safeguarding children can be a valuable source of support in undertaking this.

3.25 It may be helpful to invite a colleague, not involved in the clinical care of the child, to discuss the case on an anonymous basis and/or review the notes or to give an opinion as to whether any organic condition may have been overlooked. Likewise a general or community paediatrician may wish to discuss the case with a paediatrician who has knowledge and experience of relevant rare disorders.

3.26 **Clinical Medical Directors of paediatric services should ensure robust arrangements are in place in their NHS Trusts, Foundation Trusts or PCTs to enable consultant paediatricians to have access to teams within their Trust and across to other clinical networks outside their organisations, to discuss clinical concerns about identification, diagnosis and clinical management of fabricated or induced illness cases.**

3.27 Where the consultant has reasonable cause to suspect that a child is suffering or likely to suffer significant harm a referral should be made to children's social care (see paragraph 3.11 of this guidance). For referrals from a tertiary hospital in which the child is an inpatient this will be to children's social care local to the hospital (unless specific other local arrangements are in place between neighbouring children's social care services). This may not be the same local authority in which the child resides. If the child is an in-patient in a hospital outside their local authority area, children's social care local to the hospital has a responsibility to liaise with the appropriate one. A local authority may already be involved with the child as a 'child in need' or have had involvement in the past with either this child or other family members and know the family well. Equally, there may have been no previous involvement.

Consultants other than paediatricians

3.28 There may be occasions where concerns arise regarding FII in cases where children or young people are under the care of consultants who are not paediatricians. **As in all cases where there are child protection concerns referral to a paediatrician should be made** as set out in local policies and procedures. In the case of young people of 16-18 years, the named or designated doctor, may be able to advise about an appropriate referral.

Roles and responsibilities for nurses, midwives and health visitors

3.29 Fabricated or induced illness is an aspect of maltreatment of which all nurses, midwives and health visitors working in any setting should be aware. In the course of their work they may be in a position to recognise its signs and symptoms and risk factors.

3.30 Where a nurse, midwife or health visitor has concerns that a carer is impairing a child's health and development by fabricating or inducing illness, the nurse, midwife or health visitor should explore the presenting information to see where it is on the continuum from parental concern, over-anxiety, through to suspected significant harm. In cases where fabricated or induced illness is suspected, safeguarding children processes should be followed in accordance with Chapter 4 of this guidance.

3.31 Advice and support should be sought wherever possible from designated and named nurses/ midwives for safeguarding. It is also available from children's social care. All referrals should be made in accordance with LSCB safeguarding children procedures and local trust policies.

3.32 The nurse, midwife or health visitor may observe unusual behaviour or unexplained incidents. An accurate, contemporaneous and secure record of actual or inferred physical or behavioural observations should be kept (see paragraphs 6.24 – 6.34 on record keeping).

3.33 During the course of an assessment the nurse may be responsible for the collection of specimens such as urine or faeces. These should be collected and sent off for analysis in such a way that they cannot be interfered with (for further information see Section 5.3, *Medical Evaluation of Symptoms and Signs* in the Report of the Royal College of Paediatrics and Child Health, 2002).

3.34 Nursing, midwifery or health visiting assessments will contribute to the initial and core assessments (see paragraphs 5.24 – 5.25, *Assessment Framework*), by defining any known problems that the family is experiencing, and understanding how and if these problems have contributed to the maltreatment of the child.

3.35 When midwives are contributing to an assessment, information obtained at booking should be carefully analysed. This could include:

- the contents of the General Practitioners' referral letter (where applicable);
- information given by the mother, particularly if the woman gives a history of inexplicable illnesses; unusual complications of pregnancy, unexpected deaths in the family; family members with untreatable illnesses; or her children having complicated medical histories;

histories of failure to thrive or non accidental injuries; and if signs and symptoms reported by the mother are not observed by the midwife; and

- information available from previous maternity case notes.

Other health professionals

3.36 All other health professionals whether working with children or adults who are parents or have parenting responsibilities should be aware of the LSCB safeguarding children procedures. A range of professionals working in health care settings, for example pharmacists, physiotherapists, occupational therapists, speech and language therapists, nursery nurses and play specialists will have important roles to play in identifying and managing fabricated or induced illness in children. If, in the course of their work, these professionals have concerns about illness being fabricated or induced by a carer, they should discuss these with their clinical manager or, if the child has been referred to them, with the referring medical doctor. All health professionals should have access to further advice from the Trust's named doctor or nurse/midwife.

3.37 Some health professionals may already be working with a child when the concerns are raised and be a part of the initial assessment and decision making processes; some may become involved subsequently, often in a more in-depth assessment of the child's needs and the provision of services. Professionals such as physiotherapists, speech and language and occupational therapists, nursery nurses or play specialists are likely to be closely involved where a child's developmental progress has been impaired as a result of their illness fabrication or induction.

Roles of different health services

Universal services – General Practitioner, the primary health care team, practice-employed staff and school nurses

3.38 The GP and all members of the Primary Health Care Team (PHCT), particularly midwives, health visitors, practice nurses and school nurses are well placed to recognise the early signs and symptoms of fabricated or induced illness in a child, through their monitoring of pregnancies and child health promotion. Primary health care teams may include psychologists or counsellors. Such professionals may infrequently be involved in consultations with patients that reveal the possibility of fabricated or induced illness by the individual who is being counselled or supported.

3.39 Professionals in PHCTs may have unique knowledge of uncorroborated, odd or unusual presentations. Also, of those children who frequently attend the clinic where there is a discrepancy between the child's reported signs and symptoms and those observed, and where there is a history of abnormal illness behaviours in the family.

3.40 Such cases can pose conflicts of loyalty for primary care staff for whom the child and the parents may both be patients. Such professionals have a duty to safeguard and promote the welfare of the child. (For further information, see Joint Statement by the Department for Children,

Schools and Families and the Department of Health on the *Duties of Doctors and Other Health Professionals in Investigations of Child Abuse* dated 20 July 2007 on http://www.ecm.gov.uk/resources-and-practice/IG00251/)

3.41 **Where primary care staff, including GPs, have concerns regarding possible FII they should ensure the child is referred to a paediatrician for a paediatric assessment. This should not delay referral to children's social care when appropriate.** See Chapter 4 for more information. Named or designated professionals will be an invaluable source of help and advice.

3.42 GPs and PHCT members should consider issues of confidentiality carefully and in the context of the particular individual case with which they are dealing. They should be aware of the Government's information sharing guidance, *Information Sharing: Practitioners' guide (HM Government, 2006b)*. Where they have concerns that an illness is being fabricated or induced in a child, they should follow the child protection processes as set out in Chapter 4 of this document.

NHS Direct, walk-in centres

3.43 Children who are having illness fabricated or induced may present to NHS Direct, a walk-in centre or the primary health care team with concerns which may be related to fabricated or induced illness. Presentations may be related to common problems, for example, repeated nosebleeds or un-witnessed seizure like episodes or reports or claims which are unusual and not possible to test for such as particular allergies or concerns about emitting odd smells. It is not unusual for the carers of this group of children to be either seeking repeated attention or avoiding contact with all statutory agencies. Carers may convince the child that he or she has an illness which results in them having little or no social and educational experiences. Although not life threatening, these situations can be some of the most debilitating for children's health and development.

Child and Adolescent Mental Health Services

3.44 The roles of CAMHS professionals may include recognition of situations where emotional (psychological or psychiatric) and behavioural symptoms are being fabricated or induced. In the course of their work, professionals in Child and Adolescent Mental Health Services (CAMHS) may identify or come to suspect that fabricated or induced illnesses are being presented to them in the form of fabricated or induced emotional or behavioural symptoms. Fabricated or induced illness in mental health settings is particularly difficult to identify for a variety of reasons, not least because in some psychiatric conditions the symptoms which signify a mental health disorder in children (which is not fabricated or induced) are observed to vary in the degree to which they are present in different settings.

3.45 Specialist CAMHS professionals will also receive requests for advice from other professionals who are working with families where fabricated or induced illness is considered a possibility. This will usually be where fabricated illness or repeated presentation with different unexplained or unsubstantiated symptoms is thought to be taking place, or where the parent is seeking inappropriately invasive medical care for a proven physical illness, but may also be in the early stages of evaluating the possibility of more serious illness induction. The service will need to respond promptly in these circumstances. Help may be required to provide an opportunity for the other professionals to clarify their own thinking, and consider possible reasons for parental behaviours and anxieties, consider ways to explain and engage parents with professional concerns and provision of psychiatric expertise in considering the child's welfare and responses. CAMHS professionals may also help other professionals who are assisting parents with difficulties in their parenting roles or management of chronic illness, where these are a part of the overall situation. There may be an opportunity for some families to receive direct interventions from the specialist CAMHS service. Careful notes of these conversations and of the conclusions drawn must be kept, including key decisions such as to call a strategy meeting or initiate section 47 enquiries.

3.46   A third role for specialist CAMHS professionals is in the course of an assessment of the child and family where fabricated or induced illness is an issue. The service will receive requests from various sources, during the course of an overall assessment. The service should contribute with other professionals to the provision of an assessment as laid out in the *Assessment Framework*. Paragraphs 2.1 – 2.25 of the *Assessment Framework* describe the particular areas to be addressed during an assessment. The most important areas will be an assessment of the child's psychological functioning, in particular the child's beliefs and possible anxieties, about their state of health, ways to support and to improve this family's functioning and an assessment of the parents capacity to meet the child's needs.

3.47   A contribution to an assessment of the mental health functioning of a parent may also be made by CAMHS professionals. This may include, in addition to an assessment of family history, family functioning and parenting capacity, an initial view of the mental state a parent displays in the course of the assessment and the level of engagement he or she has achieved with the service. Here it will be important to liaise with colleagues in adult mental health services, where appropriate, undertake a joint assessment (see Falkov et al, 1998 for further discussion on joint working between adult and child and family psychiatrists).

3.48   CAMHS specialists will receive requests from various sources for treatment for families in which abuse of this kind is an issue or where a child is in need but concerns about significant harm have not been substantiated. CAMHS may need to offer assistance with parenting skills or work on relationships between family members. Individual work with children may also be appropriate. In particular, CAMHS may be able to help others recognise how the young person and their family respond to stress and that this may be by expressing concerns about physical or mental health disorders.

3.49   In circumstances where the child has suffered significant harm, CAMHS specialists may need to offer a range of interventions and services as part of the child's overall plan. This may include intensive work on family relationships and attachments and individual work with both parents and children. There may be a need to call on specialist resources beyond the capacity of many local areas. Wherever possible, CAMHS professionals should be able to use existing resources to initiate or continue treatment or children and families, in close liaison with other professionals and services.

Adult Mental Health Services

3.50   The full range of adult mental health professionals, including nurses, social workers, occupational therapists, clinical psychologists and psychiatrists, may need to be involved in an assessment and the treatment of a carer of a potentially abused child. This involvement may predate or follow the raising of concerns in relation to fabricated or induced illness in a child during the course of section 47 enquiries and subsequent actions, or following the identification of the carer's involvement in the abuse or likely abuse of a child.

3.51   Through their involvement with an adult patient, mental health professionals may become concerned about the welfare of a child. In particular, this may be if a carer is known to fabricate or induce illness in themselves or perhaps rarely to have a somatising disorder. If adult mental health professionals have concerns about a child they should discuss these concerns with a named doctor or nurse in their NHS Trust, the PCT designated doctor or nurse or with their local children's social care services.

Specialist assessments

3.52   A specialist adult psychiatric assessment may be sought when there is a moderate to high level of suspicion that a carer has been inducing symptoms or a court has made a finding of fact that such behaviour has occurred. To inform core assessments, or child protection conferences, it will be important to get an assessment from a psychiatrist who is familiar with both a) the relevant developmental and family psychiatric literature and b) the risk and mental disorder literature, especially in relation to personality disorder, since this is the diagnosis most often made in these situations. Additionally information would be expected to be sought from mental health clinicians involved in any ongoing treatment of the carer. It is, however, important to note that the presence of an adult mental disorder cannot be taken as evidence of fabrication or induction of illness in the child. The latter requires a paediatric evaluation.

3.53   Forensic or adult psychiatrists with expertise in the area should be sought to perform a specialist assessment of the presence, degree and severity of any mental illness or disorder that the carer may have, including personality disorder. The specialist assessment should draw on the risk and mental disorder literature when asked to give an opinion about risk of significant harm to a child or children who have had illness fabricated or induced.

3.54   The specialist assessment would be expected to include a full family medical history, with a developmental history of the carer, and a full obstetric history (see paragraph 6.21 on health professionals sharing information with each other). Access to the GP notes and/or the obstetric notes will be helpful. General practice notes will give some indication about how parents have interacted with healthcare professionals prior to concerns being raised about their having fabricated or induced illness in their child. It may be helpful to obtain formal personality assessments from a forensic psychiatric team or from a clinical psychologist.

3.55 A detailed case history should be summarised by the specialist assessor. Any psychiatric disorder (including personality disorder) should also be carefully described in terms of its presentation, severity and treatment. To be safe and of value in future decisions about the child's welfare, a report should attempt to set out not only the nature of any disorder but also suggestions about how best the adult carer's mental health might be managed.

3.56 Consideration should be given to external stressors in the carer's life. Some of the child abuse literature suggests that abuse to a child may be triggered by some other external stressors, especially violence within the home. Assessing psychiatrists should ask routinely about domestic violence. A significant proportion of women have experienced victimisation as adults such as domestic violence or rape. It may also be important (particularly in the context of abnormal illness behaviour) to enquire about the health of family members and/or recent bereavements.

3.57 Details of forensic history should be sought. This will not necessarily be easy with an adult who already feels under suspicion, but has not been charged with any criminal offence. Parents who are being assessed in the context of family court proceedings are likely to be defensive and hostile, and this should **not** prima facie be taken as an indication of a personality disorder or guilt.

3.58 A psychiatric inpatient assessment may be considered if the carer's mental disorder is of a severity that would preclude a community-based assessment. Those familiar with work with offenders report that people are often very defensive and in denial at the start of an investigative process, but over a period of time may be more able to acknowledge what they have done. Given that complete denial of any offending behaviour and a projection of responsibility on to others is a poor prognostic sign in terms of treatment outcome, it is very important to assess the issue of denial carefully and thoughtfully. Non-compliance with treatment may need to be a point of starting the intervention rather than a reason for abandoning it. There may be a conflict between the adult's timescales for change and the child's need for permanency. This may mean that decisions have to be made to place the child in an alternative family context before the adult's treatment has been successfully completed.

3.59 Assessing psychiatrists should be able to liaise with those assessing the child and those who have knowledge of the child's health. It will be helpful for the assessing psychiatrist to have access to the paediatric notes as well as the child's general practice notes.

3.60 As in all forensic cases it is helpful to separate out those clinicians who undertake assessments for legal proceedings, and those who offer treatment. It is helpful for an assessing psychiatrist to liaise with the treating psychiatrist during the process of completing an assessment, as the parent's response to treatment may be an important indicator of future risk of harm to the child if in the care of the parent.

3.61 If the assessing psychiatrist is being asked to comment about treatment, then this question should distinguish between treatment for the carer's psychological needs and treatment for risk improvement. These aims are not necessarily the same.

3.62 It will be helpful if the psychiatrist can take potential risk of harm explicitly into account in making recommendations. It is, however, acknowledged that there is currently an insufficient forensic evidence base to support the professional in making categorical statements or judgements about risk of harm to the child (children).

3.63 A focus of treatment which emphasises risk reduction would be consistent with other treatment innovations in forensic psychiatry and psychology, and has the advantage of transparency. However, the fact that a parent will not be reunited with their child(ren) should not be reason for not offering treatment for risk of harm. This is particularly so if the mother is of child bearing age.

Local authorities

3.64 Safeguarding and promoting the welfare of children is the responsibility of the local authority working in partnership with other public organisations, the voluntary and independent sectors, children and young people, parents and carers, and the wider community. A key objective for the local authorities is to ensure that children are protected from harm. All local authority services have an impact on the lives of children and families: this guidance recognises that those working in housing, sport, leisure and environmental health are less likely to be involved in cases of fabricated or induced illness. However, if they are involved with a child where it is suspected or known the illness is being fabricated or induced, they should follow the guidance in *Working Together* (see paragraphs 2.9 – 2.26) which sets out their roles and responsibilities more fully.

3.65 Local authorities have a duty to plan services for children in need, in consultation with a wide range of other agencies, and to publish the resulting children's services plans. The local authority is required to establish a Local Safeguarding Children Board (LSCB) – the key statutory mechanism for agreeing how the relevant organisations in each local area will cooperate to safeguard and promote the welfare of children in that locality and for ensuring the effectiveness of what they do (paragraph 3.2, *Working Together*).

3.66 Many authorities have management structures which cut across traditional departmental and service boundaries and which bring together a range of children's services. Where this guidance refers to children's social care, this indicates that part of the local authority which carries out children's social services functions.

Councils that are children's services authorities[1]

3.67 Under the Children Act 1989 LA children's social care has lead responsibility for the protection of children from harm. A key duty for the LA is to both safeguard and promote the welfare of

---

1. County level or unitary authorities are defined as children's services authorities in the Children Act 2004. Section 63 of the Act sets out the full definition.

children. Safeguarding and promoting the welfare of children has four elements: protecting children from maltreatment; preventing impairment of children's health or development; ensuring that children are growing up in circumstances consistent with the provision of safe and effective care; and undertaking that role so as to enable those children to have optimum life chances and to enter adulthood successfully (paragraph 1.18 of *Working Together*). This section which sets out the roles and responsibilities of children's social care should be read in conjunction with paragraphs 2.9 to 2.17 of *Working Together* paragraphs 5.9 to 5.15 of the *Assessment Framework*. In this supplementary guidance, the focus is on the specific responsibilities of children's social care in the management of cases where children are suffering or likely to suffer significant harm as a result of illness which has been fabricated or induced by a carer. These responsibilities fall into four main areas: assessment including section 47 enquiries, planning, provision of services and reviewing children's progress.

Assessment

3.68 Children's social care has lead responsibility for undertaking an initial assessment of a child in need. This will include circumstances in which fabricated or induced illness by a carer is suspected. Children's social care will conduct the initial assessment in conjunction with the doctor who has lead responsibility for the child's healthcare (usually a consultant paediatrician) and other relevant agencies (see paragraph 3.27).

3.69 Children's social care also has lead responsibility for any core assessment and will co-ordinate the process of systematic information gathering to build up a medical, psychiatric and social history and an understanding of the child's needs and the parents' capacities to meet the child' developmental needs. Children's social care should ensure that a comprehensive chronology of the child's history is compiled.

3.70 Children's social care should work collaboratively with all other agencies currently involved with the child and family. In addition, it is likely to be necessary to contact agencies with past involvement in order to prepare a full history of the child's health and family situation.

3.71 There must be clarity about roles and responsibilities during the assessment process and about what information can be shared with parents, including issues of timing, as well as between agencies.

3.72 Children's social care also have a duty, under section 47 of the Children Act 1989, to make enquiries if they have reasonable cause to suspect that a child in their area is suffering, or likely to suffer significant harm. This includes cases where the harm may be a result of fabricated or induced illness. These enquiries enable them to decide whether they should take any action to safeguard and promote the child's welfare. A core assessment is commenced at the point at which section 47 enquiries are initiated in a strategy discussion. The Police decide whether to instigate a criminal investigation having considered the views of other agencies (paragraphs 5.17-5.22, *Working Together*).

3.73 Children's social care are responsible for convening strategy discussions, and, when appropriate, initial and review Child Protection Conferences, in order to review the child's situation and to decide and plan any further action which may be necessary. Any agency may request a strategy meeting or child protection conference, if it has concerns that a child may be or is suffering significant harm.

Planning

3.74 An outcome of section 47 enquiries may be that the concerns are substantiated but the child is not judged to be at continuing risk of harm. A child in need plan may be developed at the conclusion of the core assessment, which will involve the child and family members as appropriate and the contributions of all agencies (paragraph 4.33, *Assessment Framework*). The plan will set out what services are to be provided by which agency, the objectives to be met if the child is to achieve optimal developmental progress, and which agency has lead responsibility for reviewing the plan at regular intervals (Figure 7, *Assessment Framework*).

3.75 If a child protection conference is held, children's social care must ensure that their staff are sufficiently senior to be able to commit the department to following through on recommendations regarding action to be taken immediately after the conference. This is particularly relevant for recommendations regarding the seeking of emergency protection or interim care orders; where the child should live; and the nature and frequency of contact with parents or other carers.

3.76 Children's social care is responsible for coordinating a multi-agency child protection plan to promote and safeguard the child's welfare. It will also act as the principal point of contact for other agencies which may want to report new or further concerns about the child.

3.77 Where the child's welfare cannot be safeguarded if he or she remains at home, children's social care may apply to the courts for a Care Order, or if the child is in immediate danger, for an Emergency Protection Order. This should involve the local authority's solicitor who has responsibility for co-ordinating the legal proceedings. Children's social care should co-ordinate, in conjunction with the responsible paediatric consultant where appropriate, further medical investigations, expert opinions, assessments and intervention, and arrange placements and contact between the child and parents. Where necessary, contact should be supervised.

Provision of services

3.78 Children's social care have a duty to safeguard and promote the welfare of children in need in their area, through the provision of services appropriate to the needs of such children and as far as is consistent with this, to promote, the upbringing of children within their families (section 17 of the Children Act 1989). They should do this by working with parents and in a way which is sensitive to the child's race, religion, culture and language. Children's social care are responsible for providing direct services as appropriate and co-ordinating all services, which are set out in the child's plan.

Reviewing

3.79 Children's social care has lead responsibility for reviewing any child protection or care plan, and if agreed by the parties, a child in need plan (paragraphs 4.32 – 4.37, *Assessment Framework*).

Local authority solicitors

3.80 If legal action is planned, a local authority solicitor will co-ordinate these proceedings. They are also able to provide advice to local authority staff on legal matters relating to the child's welfare and the nature and quality of any evidence of the child suffering or being likely to suffer significant harm, as well as advice on matters such as consent, confidentiality and disclosure of information.

Connexions – services provided under s114 of the Learning and Skills Act 2000

3.81 Connexions is currently delivered by a range of organisations including LAs. Where LAs have responsibility for the delivery of the Connexions service, the duty to make arrangements to ensure they have regard to the need to safeguard and promote the welfare of children and young people applies. Each Connexions partnership has a substantial workforce working directly with young people. The workforce includes not only professionally qualified personal advisers, but also other delivery staff working under their supervision.

3.82 The Connexions partnership (including its subcontractors) is responsible for:

- identifying, keeping in touch with and giving the necessary support to young people in their geographical area. Each young person's needs are assessed and the support and continuing contact they receive is tailored to their assessed needs. A young person may receive any combination of the following according to their needs: information, advice, guidance, counselling, personal development opportunities, referral to specialist services, and advocacy to enable them to access opportunities for funding or other services. The needs of young people from vulnerable groups such as teenage mothers, care leavers, young people supervised by Yots, and young people with learning difficulties and/or disabilities are a particular priority for Connexions partnerships

- identifying young people who may be at risk of harm and, in these cases, for alerting the appropriate authority. Connexions staff should be aware of the agencies and contacts to use to refer young people when there are concerns about them being at risk of harm, and should be aware of the way in which these concerns will be followed up

- minimising risk to the safety of young people on premises for which the Connexions partnership or their subcontractors are responsible. The partnership should maintain the necessary capacity to carry out relevant risk assessments

- ensuring that staff (including subcontractors) are aware of risks of harm to the welfare of young people and can exercise their legal, ethical, operational and professional obligations to safeguard and promote their welfare. Information sharing protocols with other agencies should give the highest priority to safeguarding and promoting the welfare of young people, and staff should comply fully with these agreements.

3.83 Where staff working in a Connexions partnership (including through sub-contract) become aware of suspicions that illness may be being fabricated or induced in a young person, they should follow this guidance. Similarly they should follow this guidance if they have concerns where providing services as part of an agreed child protection or care plan.

Children's centres, schools and further education institutions

3.84 Paragraphs 2.121 – 2.132 of *Working Together* set out the role of schools and further education institutions. *Safeguarding Children and Safer Recruitment in Education* (2006) also provides further guidance.

3.85 Guidance on safeguarding children procedures provides advice to the education service on what they should do if they have reason to believe a pupil is being harmed or is at risk from harm. Through their day-to-day contact with children, teachers and other school staff are particularly well placed to notice outward signs of harm. For pre-school children, Children's centres will have a key role to play in the identification and management of suspected cases of fabricated or induced illness. This may occur when parents give a description of the child's ill health which does not accord with the observations of children's centre staff. Although this discrepancy can do no more than raise concerns about possible significant harm, teachers, children's centre staff and all other staff should be alert to this possibility. They should know how to seek further information and to whom they should address their child welfare concerns.

3.86 Children's centre managers, in conjunction with the local authority, should ensure their centre has a clear safeguarding children policy and that all staff can demonstrate an understanding of child protection and how this relates to their role. In practice this means managers should:

- use the documentation from its Local Safeguarding Children Board;

- appoint a lead person whose job it is to ensure every member of staff is competent in their knowledge of child protection and knows what to do if they are worried that a child is being harmed and what the procedure is for reporting and recording child protection concerns;

- ensure parents are aware that staff have a duty to share child protection concerns with other professionals and agencies; and

- be ready to support children, their families and staff if a referral to children's social care or section 47 enquires were to occur.

3.87 It is important that schools do not undertake their own enquiries if they have reason to suspect possible or actual harm. They should not take action beyond that which has been agreed in the safeguarding children procedures set down by their Local Safeguarding Children Board (LSCB). Enquiries into concerns about a child's welfare are the responsibility of the appropriate local agencies such as children's social care or the police. They have the necessary professional expertise to take such enquiries forward.

3.88 Schools have an important role to play in the identification and management of suspected cases of fabricated or induced illness and further guidance is set out below. Where there are concerns about a child being given medicines inappropriately, please refer to the government's guidance on managing medicines (Department for Education and Skills and Department of Health, 2005). As with all other forms of suspected harm, teachers, children's centre staff and all other staff should refer any child welfare concerns they have to the senior member of staff with designated responsibility for child protection issues. He or she should act as a source of advice and support, and is responsible for co-ordinating action within the institution and liaising with other agencies. The designated teacher can, in turn, seek advice from their LEA senior officer with responsibility for co-ordinating action and policy on child protection. This person is also usually Local Education Authority's representative on the LSCB.

3.89 Absences from school are common and occur for many reasons including legitimate medical and hospital appointments. If fabricated or induced illness by a carer is suspected, schools should verify the reasons for the child's absences. They should also determine whether reported illness is being used by the child, for example, to avoid unpopular lessons or being bullied. It is not within the scope of this document to offer guidance in these circumstances. Such concerns should not be dismissed. On the contrary, they are very real and have an impact on pupils' behaviour and academic performance. Schools should have their own procedures in place for dealing with such situations. (see *Advice and guidance to Schools and Local Authorities on managing pupil attendance* (Department for Education and Skills, *2006)*.) When an illness is genuine the schools' own sickness procedures will apply.

Identification of fabricated or induced illness

3.90 Fabricated or induced illness is often, but not exclusively, associated with emotional abuse. There are a number of factors that teachers and other school staff should be aware of that can indicate that a pupil may be at risk of harm. Some of these factors can be:

- frequent and unexplained absences from school, particularly from PE lessons;

- regular absences to keep a doctor's or a hospital appointment; or

- repeated claims by parent(s) that a child is frequently unwell and that he/she requires medical attention for symptoms which, when described, are vague in nature, difficult to diagnose and which teachers/ early years staff have not themselves noticed eg headaches, tummy aches, dizzy spells, frequent contact with opticians and/or dentists or referrals for second opinions.

3.91 The child may disclose some form of ill-treatment to a member of staff or might complain about multiple visits to the doctor. Either the child or his or her parent(s) may relate conflicting or patently untrue stories about illnesses, accidents or deaths in the family. Where there is a sibling in the same institution, teachers/ early years staff should discuss their concerns with each other to see if children of different ages in the same family are presenting similar concerns. If they are, it is likely that more than one child in the family is affected. The school nurse may also be able to contribute to the initial evaluation of concerns.

3.92 There are also circumstances under which a child will demonstrate his or her anxiety or insecurity by presenting symptoms of an illness that will allow them to stay at home. This may occur as a response to family problems, for example, as a reaction to a parent is ill, who has been in hospital or, after a divorce or separation, but this is not an aspect of fabricated or induced illness.

Management of fabricated or induced illness

3.93 Where a teacher or other member of staff has reasonable cause to believe a child is at risk from, or is the subject of, fabricated or induced illness, the institution's safeguarding children procedures apply. This will require the member of staff to refer his or her concerns to the senior member of staff with designated lead for child protection who is then responsible for making a referral to children's social care.

3.94 Schools and early years staff should, in particular, be alert to any significant change in the child's physical or emotional state, in his or her behaviour or failure to develop and draw these to the attention of the designated senior member of staff.

3.95 It is helpful if, prior to referral to the designated senior staff member, the member of staff concerned can present a diary of events, including a record of absences and the reasons for absence given by the parent (where known). He or she should also listen carefully to what the child relates and should record any discussions with the child, including quotes of what the child said. The time, date, place and names of any people who were also present at the time should also be recorded.

3.96 As stated above, neither schools, early years' settings nor members of staff, should carry out their own enquiries. After the designated senior staff member has referred a concern, it is for those agencies with a professional interest, i.e. children's social care services or the police to take matters forward in line with LSCB safeguarding children procedures. The designated senior member of staff is normally invited to attend any strategy discussions or child protection conferences. The conference should notify the designated teacher of the extent to which the child's parents have been notified of the concern for the child and what information can be shared. All parties should follow the decisions made at the strategy discussions and conferences, in particular in relation to what information may be shared.

3.97 If, in the course of an inspection, inspectors become concerned about the possibility that a child may be having illness fabricated or induced, they should follow OFSTED's child protection procedures.

Police

3.98 This section should be read in conjunction with paragraphs 2.97 – 2.105 of *Working Together* which set out the principles applying to the police role in child protection investigations.

3.99 Any suspected case of fabricated or induced illness may also involve the commission of a crime, and therefore the police should always be involved in accordance with paragraphs 5.17-5.22 of *Working Together*. Events such as intentional smothering or poisoning are clearly criminal assaults, but more subtle forms of child abuse, such as wilfully interfering with feeding lines or causing unnecessary medical intervention to be undertaken, may also be criminal acts.

3.100 The police should be alerted to suspected cases of fabricated and especially induced illness as early as possible. It may be crucial for any ongoing criminal investigation that the carer is not made aware of the child protection concerns. There are many low key enquiries which can be made by the police before any proactive investigation is launched. At this stage, i.e. before suspicions are confirmed, the responsible consultant for the child's health (usually a paediatrician) should retain the lead role for the child's health, and the priority of police officers should be to assist the paediatrician, where relevant and appropriate in reaching an understanding of the child's health status. The balance may change when it becomes clear whether or that a crime appears to have been committed. In such circumstances, the police will need to ensure the rights of the suspect are upheld and that evidence is gathered in a fair and appropriate way.

3.101 The Police Service is the prime agency for gathering evidence in connection with criminal cases. There is sometimes reluctance on the part of doctors to involve the police, but it must be remembered that all professionals should be working towards the same goal, i.e. securing the safety of the child. It may well be that enquiries made by the police assist in identifying that the underlying explanation for the child's symptoms is not related to harm caused by a carer. In any case, the police should work within the multi-agency framework, and all relevant information should be shared with those professionals treating the child. Any evidence of child abuse gathered by the police will normally be available for use by the local authority in any care proceedings.

3.102 The police use technical means to gather evidence in many types of criminal enquiry, and it may be appropriate to use such methods, for example covert video surveillance, in cases of suspected fabricated or induced illness. In a case, where this is indicated as appropriate by the multi-agency strategy discussion, the police will supply any equipment required and be responsible for monitoring and managing the process. The police, like other public authorities, are bound by the Human Rights Act 1998 and the Regulation of Investigatory Powers Act 2000. Any operations within this context therefore will be carefully controlled and police managers will be fully accountable. **Doctors or other professionals should not independently carry out covert video surveillance**. If the suspicion of child abuse is high enough to consider the use of such a technique, the threshold must have been passed to involve the police and children's social care services. The National Crime Faculty provides confidential good practice advice for police officers.

3.103 The police should carry out any work within a hospital sensitively and delicately, with any disruption to normal ward life being kept to a minimum. Any arrest or interview in a hospital setting should be carried out as sensitively as possible, ideally using plain clothes officers, to avoid disruption to patients and staff. The inter-agency management team should, if possible, consider the arrest strategy well in advance of it being carried out.

3.104 Irrespective of what evidence is likely to be used in the Civil Court or the Criminal Court or both, it must be gathered to the highest standards. When the police are involved in a situation where induced or fabricated illness is suspected, even greater care should be taken to ensure that the investigation is thorough and professional, and led by an experienced senior investigating officer.

Probation services

3.105 The range of roles and responsibilities of the probation service in relation to safeguarding children is set out in paragraphs 2.106 – 2.107 of *Working Together*. Probation services have a statutory duty to supervise offenders effectively in order to reduce re-offending and protect the public. In the execution of that duty probation officers will be in contact with, or supervising, a number of men (and, to a far lesser extent, women) who have convictions for offences against children. A very small number may have been convicted for offences relating to the fabrication or induction of illness in a child. It is, however, more likely that probation officers may become aware of past events which cause them to suspect that the person they are supervising has been involved in the fabrication or induction of illness in a child. For example, they may become aware that a child died in suspicious circumstances and suspect the child had been intentionally smothered rather than dying from natural causes.

3.106 Where probation officers, in the normal course of their work in the community, become concerned about the safety of a child or children they should work closely with the police, children's social care services and other relevant organisations to assess the risk of harm posed to children by known and suspected offenders.

Voluntary and independent sectors

3.107 Voluntary organisations and independent sector providers play an important role in delivering services to children in need. They provide a wide range of supportive services and may be involved in providing these after fabricated or induced illness has been identified.

3.108 The range of roles fulfilled by these organisations means that they should have clear guidance and procedures in place to ensure that, when they are concerned a child may be suffering significant harm, appropriate referrals are made in accordance with LSCB safeguarding children procedures. Staff and volunteers should be trained so that they are aware of the indicators of possible harm in the children with whom they are working. This general responsibility also applies in instances where a concern arises that a child may be subject to maltreatment due to fabricated or induced illness.

Children and Family Court Advisory and Support Service (CAFCASS)

3.109 The roles of CAFCASS Guardians and Reporting Officers are set out in paragraphs 2.134 – 2.137 of *Working Together*. Within CAFCASS, officers of the service undertake a range of functions, including involvement in care and related proceedings under the Children Act 1989, and proceedings under adoption legislation. Their duties are to safeguard and promote the welfare of children who are the subject of proceedings by providing advice to the court as an independent professional, not as an officer of the court. In care-related applications where the child is a party to the proceedings, the officer appoints a solicitor to represent the child and is responsible for instructing the solicitor.

3.110 In private law proceedings the officer of the service is referred to in court rules as the *'children's guardian'*. This role is limited to the duration of the court proceedings, including any appeal that might be lodged. In each case the *children's guardian* should exercise discretion over how best to undertake enquiries, assess information, consult a range of professionals and report to the court at interim hearings, directions appointments and at the final hearing.

3.111 Officers of the service have a statutory right to access and take copies of local authority records relating to the child concerned and any application under the Children Act 1989. That power also extends to other records which relate to the child and the wider functions of the local authority or records held by an authorised body (i.e. the NSPCC) which relate to that child.

3.112 CAFCASS Officers of the service appointed by the court as a *children's guardian* should always be invited to formal planning meetings convened by the local authority in respect of the child. This includes statutory reviews of children who are looked after by the local authority and child protection conferences and relevant Adoption Panel meetings. The conference chair should ensure that all those attending such meetings, including the child and any family members, understand the role of the CAFCASS Officer.

Family Justice Courts

3.113 In the event that proceedings are issued for a Care or Supervision Order under the Children Act 1989 (see paragraph 3.75), all professionals involved should adopt an inter-disciplinary approach to their work. An awareness of the tasks and responsibilities of other professionals increases the possibility of consensus on issues, if not on outcome. These considerations are of particular importance in those cases where difficult issues of fact or opinion have been referred to more than one expert.

3.114 If good practice issues or difficulties seem to recur in any locality, they may be referred to the Designated Judge of the relevant Care Centre or to the Business Committee which the Judge chairs.

The Armed Services

3.115 In England, local authorities have the statutory responsibility for the safeguarding and promoting the welfare of the children of service families in the UK.

3.116 When service families (or civilians working with the armed forces) are based overseas, the responsibility for safeguarding and promoting the welfare of children is vested with the MoD who fund the British Forces Social Work Service (Overseas). This service is contracted to SSAFA-FH, who provide a fully qualified Social Work and Community Health service in major overseas locations (for example, Germany and Cyprus). For further discussion on Service Families based overseas, see paragraphs 2.138 – 2.114 of *Working Together*.

Children of foreign nationals

3.117 Where safeguarding concerns regarding fabricated or induced illness are raised about children who are foreign nationals, the procedures set out in this guidance apply.

Chapter Four
Managing individual cases

Introduction

4.1 All parents demonstrate a range of behaviours in response to their children being ill or being perceived as ill. Some may become more stressed or anxious than others. Their responses may in part relate to their perceptions of illness and to their expectations of the medical profession. Health professionals are taught to listen to the concerns of parents about their children's health and to act on these. Part of their role is not only to treat the sick child but also, in collaboration with other professionals, to assist parents to respond appropriately to the state of their children's health. Further guidance on sharing information between professionals is found in *Information Sharing: Practitioners' guide* (HM Government, 2006b).

4.2 Some children may not be unwell but their parents need reassurance that they are indeed well, whilst others may experience continuing difficulty in recognising that their child is healthy and exhibiting normal childhood behaviours (for further discussion see Eminson, 2000a and 2000b; Eminson and Postlethwaite, 1992). Some parents can be helped to interpret and respond appropriately to their child's actions and behaviours, whilst others may continue to be anxious and/or are unable to change their beliefs. It is this latter group of parents who are more likely to present their children for medical examination although the children are healthy. Skilled professional intervention is likely to enable most parents to learn how to interpret their child's state of health and manage their own anxieties. There may be some parents for whom such early interventions are ineffective. These parents may have particular needs which result in them persistently presenting their child(ren) as ill and seeking investigations and medical treatments. They may benefit from a multi-agency approach to intervention. For those children who may be children in need under the Children Act 1989, the referral and initial assessment processes set out in paragraphs 4.14 – 4.22 should be followed.

4.3 For a small number of children, concerns will be raised when it is considered that the health or development of a child is likely to be significantly impaired or further impaired by the actions of a carer or carers having fabricated or induced illness. Where the impairment is such that there are concerns the child is suffering or is likely to suffer significant harm the guidance set out in this chapter should be followed.

Concerns about possible FII

4.4   **This chapter should be read in conjunction with Chapter 5 in *Working Together*.** In this supplementary guidance, the focus is on specific issues which relate to situations where there are concerns that a child is suffering or likely to suffer significant harm as a result of having illness fabricated or induced by their carer. These concerns may be raised by a number of different types of professionals or, more rarely, by family members or members of the public.

4.5   Concerns may arise about possible fabricated or induced illness when:

- reported symptoms and signs found on examination are not explained by any medical condition from which the child may be suffering; or

- physical examination and results of medical investigations do not explain reported symptoms and signs; or

- there is an inexplicably poor response to prescribed medication and other treatment; or

- new symptoms are reported on resolution of previous ones; or

- reported symptoms and found signs are not seen to begin in the absence of the carer; or

- over time the child is repeatedly presented with a range of signs and symptoms; or

- the child's normal, daily life activities are being curtailed, for example school attendance, beyond that which might be expected for any medical disorder from which the child is known to suffer.

4.6   There may be a number of explanations for these circumstances and each requires careful consideration and review. A full developmental history and an appropriate developmental assessment should be carried out. **Consultation with peers, named or designated professionals or colleagues in other agencies will be an important part of the process of making sense of the underlying reason for these signs and symptoms.** The characteristics of fabricated or induced illness are that there is a lack of the usual corroboration of findings with symptoms or signs, or, in circumstances of proven organic illness, lack of the usual response to proven effective treatments. It is this puzzling discrepancy which alerts in particular the medical clinician to possible harm being suffered by the child.

4.7   Concerns may be raised by professionals other than medical clinicians, such as nurses, teachers or social workers who are working with the child. For example, in a school or nursery setting the staff may not observe any fits in a child who is described by a parent to be having frequent fits during the day whilst in their care. In addition, professionals working with the child's parents may be being given information by the parent about the child or observe the child directly and note discrepancies between what they are told about the child's health and development and what they see themselves. For example, mental health professionals may identify a child being drawn into the parent's illness behaviour by having signs and symptoms described by the parent which replicate their own medical/psychiatric problems.

4.8 Professionals who have concerns about a child's health should discuss these with the child's GP or if the child is known to a hospital service, the consultant paediatrician responsible for the child's health care (see Chapter 3). **If any professional considers their concerns about fabricated or induced illness are not being taken seriously or responded to appropriately, they should discuss these with their local named or designated doctor or nurse.**

Medical evaluation

4.9 Signs and symptoms of illness present in a child may be suggestive of fabricated or induced illness (see paragraphs 3.10 – 3.17). The reasons for these may prove difficult to understand for a variety of reasons. Professionals should remain open to all possible explanations.

4.10 Where there are concerns about possible fabricated or induced illness the signs and symptoms require careful medical evaluation by a paediatrician(s). For children who are not already under the care of a paediatrician, the child's GP should make a referral to a paediatrician, preferably one with expertise in the specialism which seems most appropriate to the reported signs and symptoms. Tests and their results should be fully and accurately recorded, including those with negative results. It is important to ensure these records are not tampered with or results altered in the child's notes: also, that the name of the person reporting any observations about the child is recorded clearly in the child's notes and dated (refer also to paragraphs 3.15-3.16).

4.11 Where, following a set of medical tests being completed, a reason can not be found for the reported or observed signs and symptoms of illness, further specialist advice and tests may be required. Normally, the consultant responsible for the child's care will tell the parent(s) that they do not have an explanation for the signs and symptoms. The parental response to this information should be recorded. The consultant would then set out the next steps, including what further assessments/investigations/tests (perhaps in a more specialist setting) are required to tease out the possible explanations. Parents should be kept informed of findings from these medical investigations but at no time should concerns about reasons for child's signs and symptoms be shared with the parents if this information would jeopardise the child's safety. The child should continue to receive appropriate health care and support should continue to be provided to the child's carers by health professionals.

4.12 Ensuring a medical evaluation takes into account what children are saying is always important. In the case of suspected FII it is equally important, but can be complicated by some parents' reluctance to leave the child. This reluctance to allow their child to be talked to by a clinician has to be balanced against the need to see the child on their own in order to ensure the child's welfare. Every effort should be made to see the child without the parent being present. Some children may be competent to make their own decisions on this matter.

4.13 There may be times when a member of staff is responsible for the unexplained or inexplicable signs and symptoms in a child. This should be borne in mind when considering how to manage the child's care. Any such concerns about a member of staff should be discussed with the relevant named or designated professional in accordance with the LSCB safeguarding children procedures[2].

---

2. Specific advice for dealing with allegations against staff is published in *Working Together (2006)*.

Referral

4.14 LA children's social care services have particular responsibilities for children whose health or development may be impaired without provision of services, or who are disabled (defined in the Children Act 1989 as children 'in need'). When a parent, professional or another person contacts LA children's social care services with concerns about a child's welfare, it is the responsibility of LA children's social care services to clarify with the referrer (including self referrals from children and families):

- The nature of the concerns;

- How and why they have arisen; and

- What appear to be the needs of the child and family.

4.15 In response to the referral, LA children's social care services should decide on the next steps of action. This initial consideration of the case should address – on the basis of the available evidence – whether there are concerns about either the child's health and development or actual and/or potential harm that justifies an initial assessment to establish whether the child is a child in need, the nature of any services required and whether a more detailed core assessment should be undertaken. The flow charts at the end of this chapter illustrate the processes for safeguarding and promoting the welfare of children (see pages 57-62).

4.16 **These same processes, set out through** *Working Together to Safeguard Children* **(2006) should be followed when a possible explanation for the signs and symptoms of illness is that they may have been fabricated or induced by a carer.** This referral to children's social care may follow an evaluation of the child's signs and symptoms whilst an hospital in-patient; it may be as a result of concerns held by professionals working with the child or it may be as a result of concerns held by a member of the public who knows the child. While professionals should seek, in general, to discuss any concerns about a child's welfare with the family and, where possible, seek their agreement to making a referral to children's social care, **this should only be done where such discussion and agreement-seeking will not place a child at increased risk of significant harm** (see paragraph 5.16, *Working Together*). Decisions should be agreed between the referrer and the recipient of the referral, in line with LSCB safeguarding children procedures, about what the parents will be told, by whom and when.

4.17 Children's social care should decide and record, within one working day what response is necessary. From the point of referral, all professionals involved with the child and children's social care should work together. Lead responsibility for action to safeguard and promote the child's welfare lies with the latter. Any suspected case of fabricated or induced illness may involve the commission of a crime, and therefore the police should always be involved in accordance with *Working Together* (paragraphs 5.17-5.22). It is expected that the paediatric consultant responsible for the child's healthcare is the lead health professional and therefore has lead responsibility for all decisions pertaining to the child's healthcare (if a child is known to a GP but not to a paediatrician, it is important that a GP referral is made to a paediatrician and she or he assumes lead responsibility for the child's health – see paragraph 4.10). In order to safeguard and promote the child's welfare it is important that all three disciplines (i.e. health, LA social care services and the police) work closely together in making and taking forward decisions about future action, recognising each other's roles and responsibilities. All decisions about what information should be shared with the parents, when and by whom should be taken jointly in line with LSCB safeguarding children procedures. In all cases where the police are involved, the decision about when to inform the parents (about referrals from third parties) will have a bearing on the conduct of police investigations (see paragraph 5.20 of *Working Together*).

4.18 Referrals under section 17 of the Children Act 1989 may lead to no further action, or to an initial assessment of the needs and circumstances of the child and the provision of services or other help. If children's social care decides to take no further action at this stage, feedback should be provided to the referrer. In the case of referrals from members of the public, this should be done in a manner that respects the confidentiality of the child. Sometimes it may be apparent that emergency action should be taken at this stage to safeguard a child (see paragraph 3.24 of *Working Together*). Such action may be necessary when a child's life is in danger, for example, through poisoning or toxic substances being introduced into the child's blood stream. Emergency action should normally be preceded by an immediate strategy discussion between the police, children's social care, health and other agencies as appropriate. The legal team from children's social care should also be included.

Initial assessment under section 17 of the Children Act 1989

4.19 An initial assessment under section 17 of the Children Act 1989, is undertaken to determine "whether the child is in need, the nature of any services required, and whether a further, more detailed core assessment should be undertaken" (paragraph 3.9, *Assessment Framework*). The initial assessment should be carefully planned, with clarity about who is doing what, as well as when and what information is to be shared with the parents. The child should be seen by a social worker, and his or her wishes and feelings ascertained and taken account of in future plans.

4.20 Children's social care has lead responsibility for undertaking an initial assessment in conjunction with all other relevant agencies. The initial assessment should follow the guidance set out in the *Assessment Framework* (paragraphs 3.9 – 3.10) and be concluded within a maximum of 7 working days from the date of the referral (paragraph 3.9). Its timing and operation should be undertaken in collaboration with the lead paediatric consultant who is responsible for the child's health care (or a consultant's deputy nominated specifically for this case under consultant supervision). It should cover the dimensions within the three domains of the *Assessment Framework* (see Figure 1) and address the four questions set out in paragraph 5.38 of *Working Together*:

- "What are the developmental needs of the child?

- Are the parents able to respond appropriately to the child's identified needs? Is the child being adequately safeguarded from significant harm, and are the parents able to promote the child's needs and the child's developmental progress?

- What impact are the family functioning and history, the wider family and environmental factors having on the parents' capacity to respond to their child's needs and the child's developmental progress?

- Is action required to safeguard and promote the welfare of the child?"

FIGURE 1: ASSESSMENT FRAMEWORK

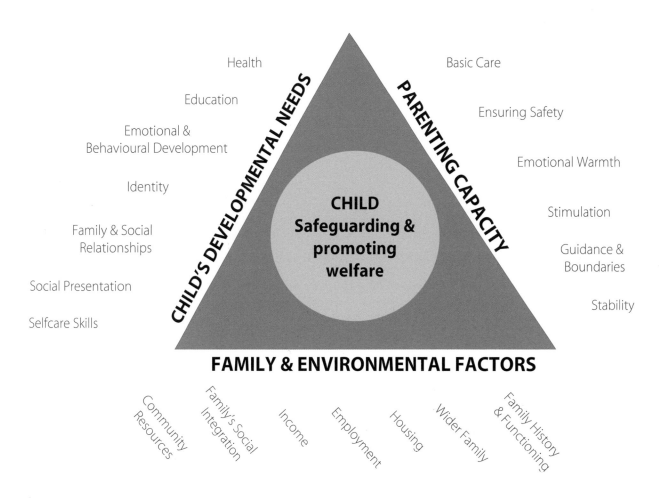

4.21 The time taken to complete the initial assessment may be very brief if it quickly becomes clear that there is reasonable cause to suspect the child is suffering or is likely to suffer significant harm. This may occur, for example, when toxicology results indicate the presence of medication that had not been prescribed. In some instances, the child's circumstances may require a more in-depth core assessment under section 17 of the Children Act 1989 (paragraph 3.11, *Assessment Framework*) before any decision can be reached about whether the criteria are met for initiating a section 47 enquiry. In addition, during the course of providing services to a child and family, concerns may be raised about the possibility of illness being fabricated or induced.

4.22 On completion of the initial assessment, children's social care together with the paediatric consultant responsible for the child's health care (or nominee) should decide on the next course of action. At this stage careful consideration should be given to what the parents should be told, when and by whom, taking account of the child's welfare (paragraph 5.45 of *Working Together*). Concerns should not be raised with a parent if it is judged that this action will jeopardise the child's safety.

Next steps

4.23 No suspected actual or likely significant harm. The child may be a child in need and it may be appropriate to undertake a core assessment in order to determine what help may benefit the child and family. Alternatively, services may be offered based on the findings of the initial assessment. It may be helpful for relevant professionals to discuss the findings of the initial assessment to inform decisions about what types of services, including a more in-depth assessment, it would be appropriate to offer. Decisions about further action should be discussed with the parents in the light of the findings of the initial assessment and consideration of what would be most helpful to the child and family.

4.24 If at any point in the core assessment or later in the course of professional involvement with the child and family, there is reasonable cause to suspect a child is suffering or is likely to suffer significant harm, a strategy discussion should be initiated.

4.25 Suspected actual or likely significant harm. Where the initial assessment identifies that the child is suspected to be suffering, or is likely to suffer significant harm, children's social care is required by section 47 of the Children Act 1989 to make enquiries, to enable the local authority to decide whether it should take any action to safeguard and promote the child's welfare. Where a criminal offence may have been committed against a child the police should be involved at the earliest opportunity. This will enable children's social care and the police to consider jointly how to proceed in the best interests of the child.

4.26 It is the responsibility of children's social care in the local authority area in which the child is currently located to initiate a strategy discussion or to apply for an application for an emergency protection order (under section 44 of the Children Act 1989) unless appropriate alternative arrangements have been made with the responsible local authority. If the child is normally resident in another local authority, the one in which the child is currently found should negotiate a transfer of statutory responsibility to the child's local authority of residence and agree how the child's case will be managed before relinquishing lead responsibility for the child's safety and welfare.

4.27 Careful thought should be given to what parents are told, when and by whom, at the point it is decided to hold a strategy discussion. Children's social care should involve the police, the child's paediatric consultant and GP, the senior ward nurse (if the child is an in-patient) and other relevant professionals in making these decisions.

Immediate protection

4.28 If at any point there is medical evidence to indicate that the child's life is at risk or there is a likelihood of serious immediate harm, an agency with statutory child protection powers **should act quickly to secure the immediate safety of the child.** Emergency action might be necessary as soon as a referral is received, or at any point in involvement with the child and their family. Alternatively, the need for emergency action may become apparent only over time as more is learned about the circumstances of a child or children. When considering whether emergency action is necessary, an agency should always consider whether action is also required to safeguard the welfare of other children in the same household (for example siblings), the household of an alleged perpetrator, or elsewhere. The nature of the abuse will be a key determining factor i.e. if it is known a child is being intentionally suffocated or poisoned then **immediate action should be taken**. If the child is subject to verbal fabrication only, and not the induction of physical signs, it is unlikely it will be necessary to act as quickly to secure the immediate safety of the child. The circumstances may change significantly if, however, the carers become aware that the professionals think the child's symptoms are being fabricated. Decisions, therefore, about possible immediate action to safeguard a child should be kept under constant review.

Strategy discussion

4.29 If there is reasonable cause to suspect the child is suffering, or is likely to suffer significant harm, children's social care should convene and chair a strategy discussion which involves all the key professionals responsible for the child's welfare. It should, at a minimum, include children's social care, the police, the paediatric consultant responsible for the child's health and, if the child is an in-patient, a senior ward nurse. It is also important to consider seeking advice from, or having present, a paediatrician who has expertise in the branch of medicine, for example respiratory, gastroenterology, neurology or renal which deals with the symptoms and illness processes caused by the suspected abuse. This would enable the medical information to be presented and evaluated from a sound evidence base. Other professionals involved with the child such as the GP, health visitor and staff from education settings should be involved also as appropriate. It may be appropriate to involve the local authority's solicitor at this meeting. Staff should be sufficiently senior to be able to contribute to the discussion of often complex information, and to make decisions on behalf of their agencies. **Decisions about undertaking covert video surveillance** (see paragraphs 6.35 – 6.40 on Covert Video Surveillance) **and keeping the records secure** (see paragraph 6.27) **should be made at a strategy discussion**.

4.30 *Working Together* does not require there to be a face to face meeting (paragraph 5.57). In this complex type of abuse, however, a meeting **is likely to be** the most effective way of professionals discussing the child's welfare and planning future action.

4.31 The strategy discussion will be used to undertake the tasks set out in paragraph 5.55 of *Working Together*. It is vital that all available information is carefully presented and evaluated, where possible its accuracy having been verified at source. Where appropriate, legal advice should be sought when evaluating the available information. Where it is decided that there are grounds to initiate a section 47 enquiry decisions should be made about:

● how a core assessment as the means to carry out an section 47 enquiry will be undertaken – what further information is required about the child and family and how it should be obtained and recorded;

● whether it is necessary for records to be kept in a secure manner in order to safeguard the child's welfare, and how this will be ensured;

- whether the child requires constant professional observation and, if so, whether or when the carer(s) should be present;

- who will carry out what actions, by when and for what purpose, in particular the planning of further paediatric assessment(s);

- any particular factors, such as the child and family's race, ethnicity and language which should be taken into account;

- the needs of siblings and other children with whom the alleged abuser has contact;

- the nature and timing of any police investigations, including the analysis of samples. This will be particularly pertinent if covert video surveillance is being considered, as this will be a task for which the police should have responsibility; and

- the needs of the parents or carers.

4.32 More than one strategy discussion may be necessary. This is likely where the child's circumstances are very complex and a number of discussions are required to consider whether and, if so, when to initiate section 47 enquiries.

Section 47 enquiries as part of a core assessment

4.33 The nature of any further medical tests will depend on the evidence available about how the signs and symptoms of illness might be being caused (see the Royal College of Paediatrics and Child Health *Report on Fabricated or Induced Illness by Carers* (2002 and being updated) for further consideration of possible medical tests).

4.34 It is important to assess the child's understanding, if old enough, of their symptoms and the nature of their relationship with each significant family member (including all caregivers), each of the caregivers' relationships with the child, the parents' relationship both with each other and with the children in the family, as well as the family's position within their community.

4.35 The core assessment should also include the systematic gathering of information about the history of the child and each family member, building on that already gathered during the course of each agency's involvement with the child. Particular emphasis should be given to health (physical and psychiatric), education and employment as well as receipt of state benefits and charitable donations relating to a disabled child, social and family functioning and any history of criminal involvement.

4.36 A range of specialist assessments may be required. For example, physiotherapists, occupational therapists, speech and language therapists and child psychologists may be involved in specific assessments relating to the child's developmental progress; child and adolescent and adult mental health professionals may be involved in assessments of individuals or of families.

4.37 Careful and detailed note taking by all staff, including health professionals, is very important for any subsequent police investigation or court action. Any unusual events should be recorded and a distinction should be made between events reported by the carer and those actually witnessed by staff from the time they began. Records should be timed, dated and signed. Most importantly, records should be kept in a secure manner so that they cannot be accessed by unauthorised persons.

Criminal investigation

4.38 The police have a key role in assisting health and children's social care staff understand the reasons for the child's signs and symptoms of illness. Whereas the police investigations may produce conclusive evidence of maltreatment, they may also confirm that the carer is not responsible for causing the child's condition. In this later situation, the police may be involved in investigating who is responsible or, if there is not evidence of a crime being committed healthcare staff can continue looking for a medical problem which arises from an intrinsic illness within the child rather than from externally induced or invented causes.

4.39 The nature and timing of any criminal investigations will depend on the medical evidence. Whether or not police investigations reveal grounds for instigating criminal proceedings, any evidence gathered by the police should be available to other relevant professionals to inform discussions about the child's welfare.

4.40 In cases where the police obtain evidence that a criminal offence has been committed by the parent or carer, and a prosecution is contemplated, it is important that the suspect's rights are protected by adherence to the Police and Criminal Evidence Act 1984. **This would normally rule out, for example, the suspect being confronted with the evidence by a paediatrician or any other personnel from the statutory agencies, except for the police, which is the lead investigative agency.**

4.41 Many of the children who have had illness fabricated or induced will be too young to be interviewed as part of any criminal investigation. If a decision is made to undertake an interview the guidance set out in *Achieving Best Evidence in Criminal Proceedings: Victims and Witnesses and Using Special Measures* (Criminal Justice System, 2007) should be followed.

The outcome of section 47 enquiries

Concerns not substantiated

4.42 Medical tests may identify a medical condition which explains the child's signs and symptoms and, therefore, no further safeguarding action may be considered necessary. In this situation, it is important to discuss with the parents, drawing on knowledge of the implications of the medical condition for the child and family members' lives, what further help or support they may require. This may be related to the child's state of health or to more general matters.

4.43 There may be situations where concerns remain about significant harm and where no tests or assessments have identified a clear explanation for the child's signs and symptoms of illness, or where there is a lack of independent evidence of their existence even when the child is constantly observed, or separated from the carer. This is more likely to be where parents report the child is having problems of a non-specific nature, such as aches and pains, or allege allergies to foods or to their environment. There could be many explanations for these symptoms, including that they are being fabricated. For these children, it is important to try to understand their origin and consider whether help is required. In particular, it is important to ensure that the child's daily life and normal activities are not being unnecessarily affected or limited. It may be that the child's health will require ongoing monitoring to see how it progresses. If problems have been recognised during the assessment process, the family may want to receive help, for example, with parenting difficulties or with improving the family's ways of relating to each other. In addressing wider family issues, it may be that the child's wellbeing improves.

Concerns substantiated, but child is not judged to be at continuing risk of significant harm

4.44 There may be substantiated concerns that a child has suffered significant harm, but it is agreed between the agencies involved with the child and family, that a plan for ensuring the child's future safety and welfare can be developed and implemented without the need for a child protection conference or a child protection plan (see paragraph 5.75, *Working Together*). For example, the carer may have taken full responsibility for the harm they have caused the child or the family's circumstances may have changed. The development of the plan may, however, require a core assessment to be completed. In these circumstances, the child's health and development would require careful monitoring by a paediatrician or other health professional over time with milestones for progress clearly set out in the child in need plan. The nature and purpose of this monitoring by health and/or other agencies should be clearly explained to the child, as appropriate, and the parents.

4.45 **Children's social care, in consultation with other agencies, should take carefully any decision not to proceed to a child protection conference where it is known that a child has suffered significant harm as a result of fabricated or induced illness.** *"A suitably experienced and qualified social work manager within LA children's social care should endorse the decision. Those professionals and agencies who are most involved with the child and family, and those who have taken part in the section 47 enquiry, have the right to request that LA children's social care convene a child protection conference if they have serious concerns that a child may not otherwise be adequately safeguarded. Any such request that is supported by a senior manager, or a named or designated professional, should normally be agreed. Where there remain differences of view over the necessity for a conference in a specific case, every effort should be made to resolve them through discussion and explanation, but as a last resort LSCBs should have in place a quick and straightforward means of resolving differences of opinion"* (paragraph 5.78, *Working Together*).

Concerns substantiated and child judged to be at continuing risk of significant harm

4.46 *"Where the agencies most involved judge that a child may continue to suffer, or to be at risk of suffering significant harm, LA children's social care should convene a child protection conference. The aim of the conference is to enable those professionals most involved with the child and family, and the family themselves, to assess all relevant information, and plan how to safeguard the child and promote the welfare of the child"* (paragraph 5.79, *Working Together*). This may include situations where the child's life has not been placed in immediate danger, but continuation of the fabrication or induction of illness would have major consequences for the child's long-term health or development (see paragraphs 2.15 – 2.18).

The initial child protection conference

Timing

4.47 *Working Together* states that an initial child protection conference should be held within 15 working days of the date of the strategy discussion. Paragraph 5.81 of *Working Together* states that there may need to be more than one strategy discussion in order to enable the best decisions to be taken about safeguarding the child's welfare. If more than one strategy discussion is held as part of a series of discussions, the initial child protection conference should be held within 15 working days of the last strategy discussion.

4.48 **Attendance**

- **Professional staff.** All relevant professionals who have been involved in the child's life should attend the conference, as well as those who are likely to be involved in future work with the child and family. Consideration should be given to inviting a professional who has expertise in working with children and families where a caregiver has fabricated or induced illness in a child. Their knowledge will be invaluable in helping conference members make sense of the information presented at the conference. It is also important to consider seeking advice from, or having present, a paediatric consultant who has expertise in the branch of paediatric medicine, eg respiratory, gastroenterology, neurology or renal, which deals with the symptoms and illness processes caused by the suspected abuse. This would enable the medical information to be presented and evaluated from a sound evidence base.

- **Child.** Children should be involved in the initial child protection conference in ways appropriate to their age and understanding. This includes discussions with them about the purpose of the conference and the means by which they want their wishes and feelings to be conveyed, as well as what they want said to whom. Some children may not understand what has been happening to them and may, therefore, find it difficult to understand what the professionals are telling them. Others may be very clear but may not have been able to talk to a trusted adult or may not have been listened to. All are likely to have suffered emotional abuse. This means that discussions should be carried out in a sensitive manner with the child knowing they are now safe. The safety of the child following the conference must also be carefully considered and an understanding of how it is to be ensured conveyed to the child.

- **Family members.** Parents should normally be invited to child protection conferences and helped to participate. Exceptionally, it may be necessary to exclude one or more family members from all or part of the conference. This decision should be based on considerations of ensuring the child's safety and be made by the conference chair on a case by case basis. Steps may also be required to protect professional staff from intimidation either in the conference or after it.

- It may not be possible for all family members to be present at the same time. The extent and manner of involvement of family members should be informed by what is known about them. The abusing carer may not be able to acknowledge their behaviour to their partner for fear of what this knowledge would do to their relationship. They should not be put under pressure to talk about their part in fabricating or inducing illness within the conference. The non-abusive parent may have had no knowledge of the abuse or they may have had some understanding which now makes better sense to them but not wish to discuss it at a conference. Again their need not to discuss their knowledge in such a public setting should be respected. These are matters which should be addressed in a sensitive manner outside the conference.

4.49 Information for the conference

- Each agency should contribute a written report to the conference setting out the nature of their involvement with the family. This information should be precise and, where possible, validated at its source. The child may have been seen by a number of professionals over a period of time: children's social care has responsibility for ensuring that, as far as is possible, this chronology (with special emphasis on the child's medical history) has been systematically brought together for the conference. Where the medical history is complex, this should be done in close collaboration with the paediatric consultant responsible for the child's health care. The health history of any siblings should also be considered. The chair has responsibility for ensuring that additional or contradictory information is presented, discussed and recorded at the conference.

- Careful consideration should be given to when agency reports will be shared with the child's parents. This decision will be made by the initial child protection conference chair, in consultation with the professional responsible for the each report.

4.50 Action and decisions for the conference

- The conference should decide whether the criterion set out in *Working Together*, namely that the child is at continuing risk of significant harm, and that the child is, therefore in need of a protection plan, is met. It may be decided that the child will not be the subject of a child protection plan. In this situation, consideration should be given to the child's needs and what future help would assist the parents in responding to them.

- If the child should be the subject of a child protection plan, an outline child protection plan should be developed following the guidance set out in paragraphs 5.116 and 5.117 of *Working Together*. Particular attention should be given to what steps will be necessary to safeguard the child's welfare. These will depend on the nature of the harm suffered by the child. If the child's life has been threatened by, for example, attempted smothering, poisoning or introducing noxious substances intravenously, all necessary measures should be put in place to ensure that these actions cannot take place in the future. This may mean that an application is made to the family court seeking agreement to separate the child from the abusing parent, and if possible cared for solely by the other parent, or, if the abusing parent is unwilling to leave the house, being placed in an alternative family context, or remain in hospital for further medical treatment before being well enough to be discharged. The nature of contact between the children and his or her parents must be carefully thought through to ensure it does not offer another opportunity to repeat the abuse. This may mean contact has to be closely supervised by a professional whose level of knowledge enables them to be alert to the precursors of further abusive behaviour.

- Conference participants must be clear what actions will be taken to safeguard the child immediately after the conference, as well as in the longer term. For some children it may be necessary to institute legal proceedings either immediately or soon after the conference has ended. This decision should be taken by children's social care in conjunction with its legal advisers. It is important that the doctors involved with the child's health agree to support this action, since it is their medical evidence which will form a key part of the evidence presented to a court.

- The conference should also consider what action is required to protect siblings in the family. It may be that the abusing parent transfers his or her abusive behaviour to another child in the family, once the identified child is placed in a safe environment.

- Knowledge of the parents' medical and psychiatric histories, in particular the abusing parent's, should be considered. Services for the parents maybe required immediately, if, for example, it is known that there is a history of self-harming behaviour or a likelihood of a parent attempting suicide or developing other types of psychiatric symptoms.

4.51 Action following the child becoming the subject of a child protection plan

- A key worker should be appointed from welfare agencies with statutory powers (LAs children's social care or the NSPCC) as set out in *Working Together* (see paragraphs 5.107 – 5.109). The outline child protection plan will have identified the most appropriate setting in which the child should live immediately following the conference, with whom and on what statutory basis. The plan should also have recommended the nature of contact between the child and the abusing parent, and between the child and other family members and whether it should be supervised by a professional person. These matters should be kept under constant review as the child's situation may change quickly. The conference should also agree a contingency plan which addresses the possibility that the plan agreed at the conference cannot be put into action, for example, if a court application is not successful or a parent removes the child from hospital.

- The child and family members should be provided with appropriate services whilst the core assessment is completed. The child may require further medical investigations to ascertain his or her current state of health as well as receiving ongoing treatment. This could range from intensive involvement, if the child is seriously ill as a result of their abuse, to no treatment but careful monitoring if the child has been found to have no medical problems and is healthy now that the abuse has stopped.

- Parents with a psychiatric history may require immediate help if, for example they have a history of attempting suicide or self-harming. This intervention with the parent will be part of the overall programme of work which focuses on the child's welfare.

- Information about past relationship difficulties and the nature and outcome of any previous therapeutic help should also inform decisions about how best to intervene in each family.

Core assessment

4.52 The core assessment, which will have begun at the time the section 47 enquiries commenced, should be completed within a maximum of 35 working days as set out in the *Assessment Framework*, recognising that some specialist assessments may not be able to be completed within this period. Indeed, it may only become clear that certain types of assessments are required part way through or at the end of the core assessment. This is more likely to be so when the child's needs are very complex.

4.53 The assessment should follow the guidance set out in the *Assessment Framework*. It should address:

- The child's current health status and his/her developmental progress, clarifying where possible the cause of any presenting symptoms, illness and/or developmental delay i.e. what may have been organic in origin and what is likely to have been related to abuse. It should also ascertain the child's educational, emotional and behavioural level of development as well as the nature of his or her relationship with each family member and how he or she is perceived within the family and their local community. A thorough understanding of the child's needs is necessary to inform decisions about how best to intervene.

- The developmental needs of the child's siblings should also be assessed, using the Assessment Framework, as they may also be children in need. Siblings should be involved in future therapeutic work. It is important to understand how they perceive their brother or sister's health.

- The parenting capacity of both parents should be assessed as well as that of other caregivers or potential caregivers. The latter is particularly important if consideration is being given to other family members looking after the child. Their understanding of the abuse and ability to believe the child has been abused by another member of their family will inform decisions about where the child lives and contact arrangements with family members. Other members of the family may not be able to protect the child from future harm if they do not believe abuse has occurred or where they can not guarantee the child's safety from abuse whilst in their care.

- The capacity of the abusing parent to recognise their child's needs is very important. They may not be able to recognise the damage they have done to their child's health. It is therefore often helpful for a psychiatrist with expertise in this area to meet with the parent(s).

- The histories of both parents will provide valuable information about their needs both as adults and as parents. It is important to ascertain the quality of the parents' relationship, including in situations where they are not living together. This information will inform decisions about what future work will be required with each parent individually, as a couple, as parents and as a family. It will also determine which professionals should be involved at what stages during the therapeutic process.

- An assessment of appropriate wider family members will provide information about the capacity of these adults to support the child and his/her parents. Many parents in these circumstances are isolated from their families or have withheld information about difficulties they are experiencing in their parenting role. Family patterns around illness may also be identified, for example, histories of illnesses which have not been medically identified or of a somatising behaviour.

4.54 All other professionals should liaise closely with children's social care (the lead agency) in gathering relevant historical material and integrating this within a assessment of the child's developmental needs and the capacity of their parents to respond to these needs within their wider family context. This information, including the capacity for change, should be used to inform decisions about the child's safety and future work with the child and family.

Analysis of the child's circumstances and future planning

4.55 Chapter 4 in the *Assessment Framework* describes the processes by which information obtained during the assessment can be analysed, and professional judgement used to inform decisions about how best to intervene. Paragraph 4.1 states that the conclusion of the assessment should result in:

- an analysis of the needs of the child and parenting capacity to respond appropriately to those needs within their family context;

- identification of whether and, if so, where interventions will be required to secure the welfare of the child or young person;

- a realistic plan of action, a timetable and a process for review.

4.56 The *Assessment Framework* states that "in drawing up a plan of intervention, careful distinction should be made between **judgements** about the child's developmental needs and parenting capacity and **decisions** about how best to address these at different points in time" (paragraph 4.20). It then sets out a number of factors which should be taken account of when making decisions about how best to address the child's identified needs. In cases of fabricated or induced illness these decisions should include ensuring the child is not the subject of further unwarranted medical intervention.

Intervention

4.57 Where a child has had illness fabricated or induced, the child protection plan should be carefully constructed on the basis of the findings of the assessment. Decisions about how to intervene, including what services to offer, should draw on evidence about what is likely to work best to bring about good outcomes for the child (see paragraph 5.121, *Working Together*). The core group has responsibility for developing and implementing the child protection plan within the outline plan agreed at the initial child protection conference (see paragraph 5.110 *Working Together*).

4.58 Interventions should specifically address:

- the developmental needs of the child;

- the child's understanding of what has happened to him or her;

- the abusing carer/child relationship and parental capacity to respond to the child's needs;

- the relationship between the adult carers both as adults and parents;

- family relationships; and

- the management of any presenting signs, illnesses or reports of symptoms.

4.59 A key issue will be whether the child's needs can be responded to within his or her family context, and **within timescales that are appropriate for the child**. These timescales may not be compatible with those for the carer who is in receipt of therapeutic help. This may mean a child cannot be safely cared for by this carer and has, therefore, to be living in a family setting where the carer is not present. In the longer term it may mean it would be in the best interests of the child to be placed in an alternative family context.

4.60 There is likely to be intensive activity in the period immediately following the initial child protection conference. This activity should be sustained over a significant period of time to ensure that the child's long-term developmental needs are met. As a result of interventions either the required changes will take place within the family system enabling the child to be safe and healthy within their family, or an alternative family context will have to be identified which will be able to respond to the child's ongoing needs.

4.61 Children who have had illness fabricated or induced may continue to experience the consequences of this abuse irrespective of where they are placed permanently; whether reunited with their families or placed in new families. This is particularly so in relation to their behavioural and emotional development (Bools et al, 1993). These findings suggest that therapeutic work with the child should continue, irrespective of where the child is placed, in order to ensure the needs of the child are responded to appropriately.

4.62 Interventions should address the child's physical, social and emotional needs. If the child has been very ill as a result of their abuse, he or she may require a period of hospitalisation before being well enough to be discharged. In parallel, work is likely to be necessary with family members in different groupings depending on the agreed plan; the relationship between the child and the carers responsible for the abuse (usually the child's mother); the parents' relationship with each other, with the abused child and with all their children; the family's relationships with health professionals; and individual work with the adult responsible for the abuse.

4.63 If the plan is to assess whether the child can be reunited with a carer responsible for the abuse, very detailed work will be required to help this carer develop the necessary parenting skills. For younger children this may involve learning to feed the child in a pleasant manner, to play with the child and facilitate their developmental progress, and to respond to the child's needs in an age appropriate manner. For older children, this may involve learning to interact with them as a well and healthy child, ensuring they attend school and facilitating the development of normal sibling and peer relationships. For all children, this should include the appropriate accessing of health care by their carers.

4.64 *"It is important that services are provided to give the family the best chance of achieving the required changes. It is equally important that in circumstances where the family situation is not improving or changing fast enough to respond to the child's needs, decisions are made about the long-term future of the child. Delay or drift can result in the child not receiving the help she or he requires and having their health or development impaired"* (Paragraph 4.31, *Assessment Framework*).

Child protection review conference

4.65 The child protection review conferencing and decision making processes should follow the guidance in *Working Together*. Decisions should be made on the basis of evidence of the child's developmental progress and meeting the targets set for improvement, as well as changes in the way in which the family functions. The child must be living within a safe family environment.

4.66 It has to be recognised that in families where a child has been maltreated, there are some parents who will not be able to change sufficiently within the child's timescales in order to ensure the child does not continue to suffer significant harm (Jones (1998) in Department of Heath et al (2000), paragraph 4.25). The *Assessment Framework* states that "In these situations, decisions may need to be made to separate permanently the child and parent or parents. In these circumstances decisions about the nature and form of any contact will also need to be made, in the light of all that is known about the child and the family, and reviewed throughout childhood. Key to these considerations is what is in the child's best interests, informed by the child's views (Cleaver, 2000)" (paragraph 4.25).

4.67 The *Assessment Framework* sets out criteria which have been identified as suggesting a poor outcome for reuniting children who have been maltreated with their parents (paragraph 4.26), those features which suggest there are better prospects of achieving good outcomes for children (paragraph 4.28) and those where the findings from the core assessment may provide an uncertain picture of the family's capacity to change (paragraph 4.30). These criteria should be borne in mind when assessing a family and the impact of therapeutic help on the parents' capacity to respond appropriately to the child's needs.

4.68 Outcomes for children who have had illness fabricated or induced are known to be better where the work is carried out within a clear protective framework and a sustained therapeutic programme is undertaken on a multi-agency, multi-disciplinary basis focusing on safeguarding and promoting the child's welfare (see paragraphs 2.35-2.39).

Pre-birth child protection conference

4.69 Evidence of illness having been fabricated or induced in an older sibling or another child should be carefully considered during the pregnancy of a woman who is known to have abused a child in this way. Therapeutic work may have been successfully undertaken in relation to the abuse of a previous child, but an assessment of the unborn child should be undertaken. A pregnant woman may have a history of fabricating illness herself during a previous pregnancy. This could include the fabrication of medical problems while the baby is in the womb. She may also be behaving in ways which pose risks to the health of the unborn child in the current pregnancy. A pre-birth child protection conference should be convened if, following section 47 enquiries, either the unborn child's health is considered to be at risk or the baby is likely to be at risk of harm following his or her birth.

FLOW CHART 1 – MEDICAL EVALUATION WHERE THERE ARE CONCERNS REGARDING SIGNS AND SYMPTOMS OF ILLNESS

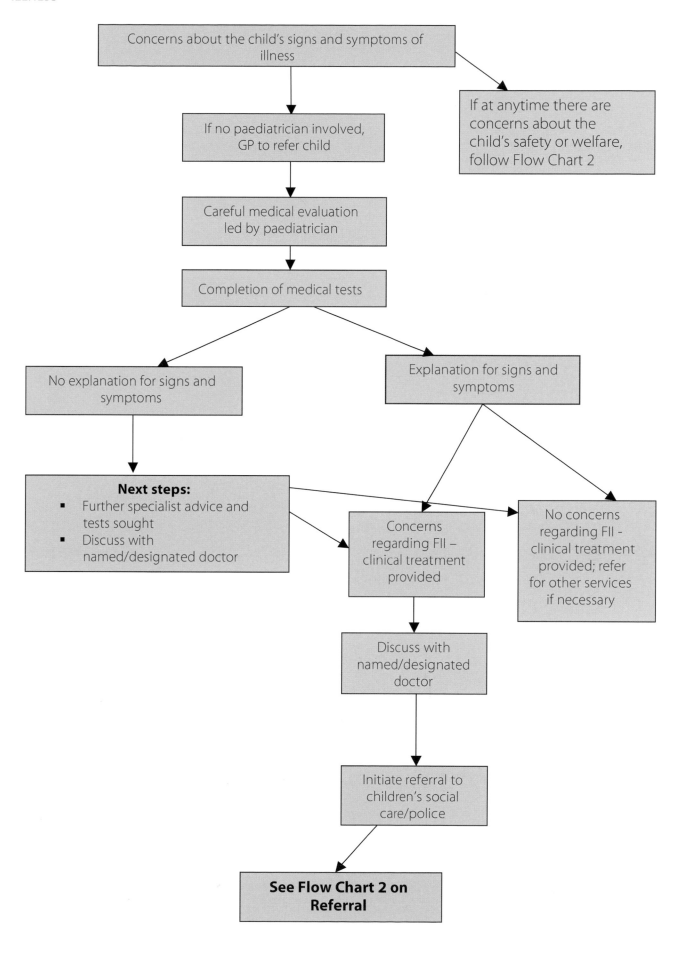

Concerns about the child's signs and symptoms of illness

If at anytime there are concerns about the child's safety or welfare, follow Flow Chart 2

If no paediatrician involved, GP to refer child

Careful medical evaluation led by paediatrician

Completion of medical tests

No explanation for signs and symptoms

Explanation for signs and symptoms

Next steps:
- Further specialist advice and tests sought
- Discuss with named/designated doctor

Concerns regarding FII – clinical treatment provided

No concerns regarding FII - clinical treatment provided; refer for other services if necessary

Discuss with named/designated doctor

Initiate referral to children's social care/police

See Flow Chart 2 on Referral

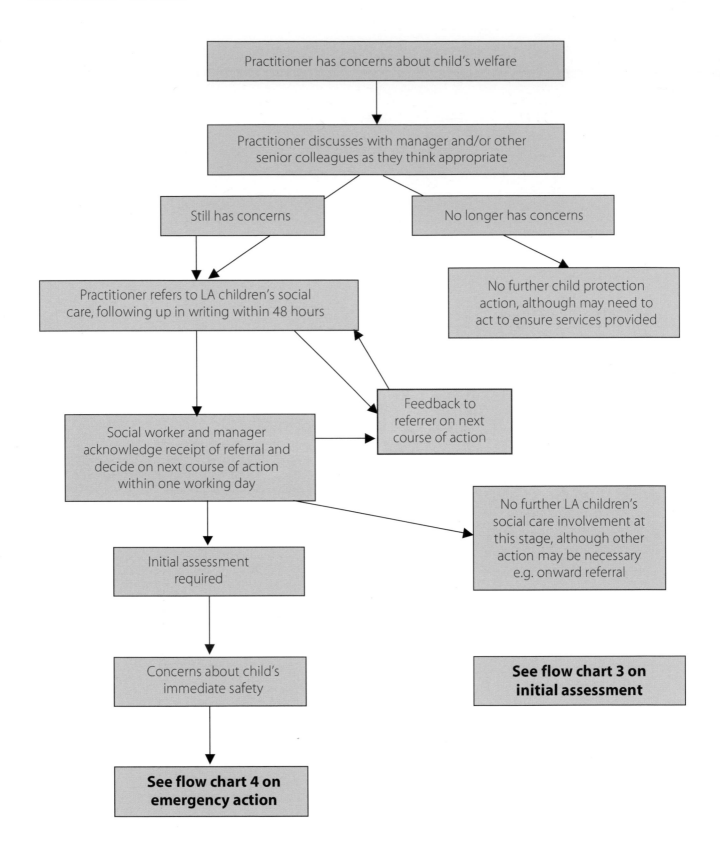

Practitioner has concerns about child's welfare

Practitioner discusses with manager and/or other senior colleagues as they think appropriate

Still has concerns

No longer has concerns

Practitioner refers to LA children's social care, following up in writing within 48 hours

No further child protection action, although may need to act to ensure services provided

Feedback to referrer on next course of action

Social worker and manager acknowledge receipt of referral and decide on next course of action within one working day

No further LA children's social care involvement at this stage, although other action may be necessary e.g. onward referral

Initial assessment required

Concerns about child's immediate safety

See flow chart 3 on initial assessment

See flow chart 4 on emergency action

FLOW CHART 3 – WHAT HAPPENS FOLLOWING INITIAL ASSESSMENT?

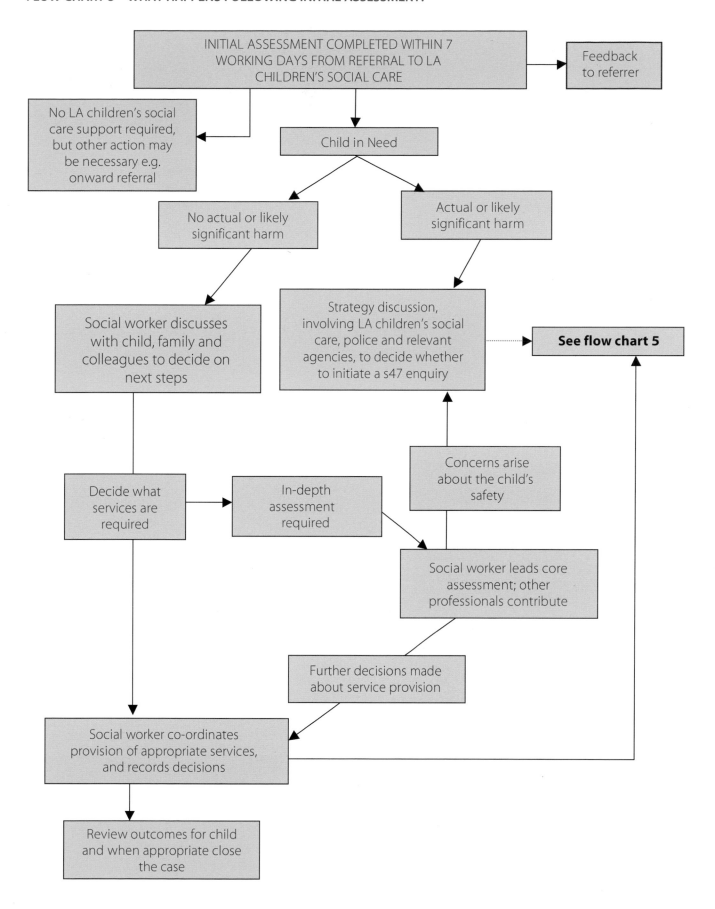

INITIAL ASSESSMENT COMPLETED WITHIN 7 WORKING DAYS FROM REFERRAL TO LA CHILDREN'S SOCIAL CARE

Feedback to referrer

No LA children's social care support required, but other action may be necessary e.g. onward referral

Child in Need

No actual or likely significant harm

Actual or likely significant harm

Social worker discusses with child, family and colleagues to decide on next steps

Strategy discussion, involving LA children's social care, police and relevant agencies, to decide whether to initiate a s47 enquiry

See flow chart 5

Decide what services are required

In-depth assessment required

Concerns arise about the child's safety

Social worker leads core assessment; other professionals contribute

Further decisions made about service provision

Social worker co-ordinates provision of appropriate services, and records decisions

Review outcomes for child and when appropriate close the case

FLOW CHART 4 – URGENT ACTION TO SAFEGUARD CHILDREN

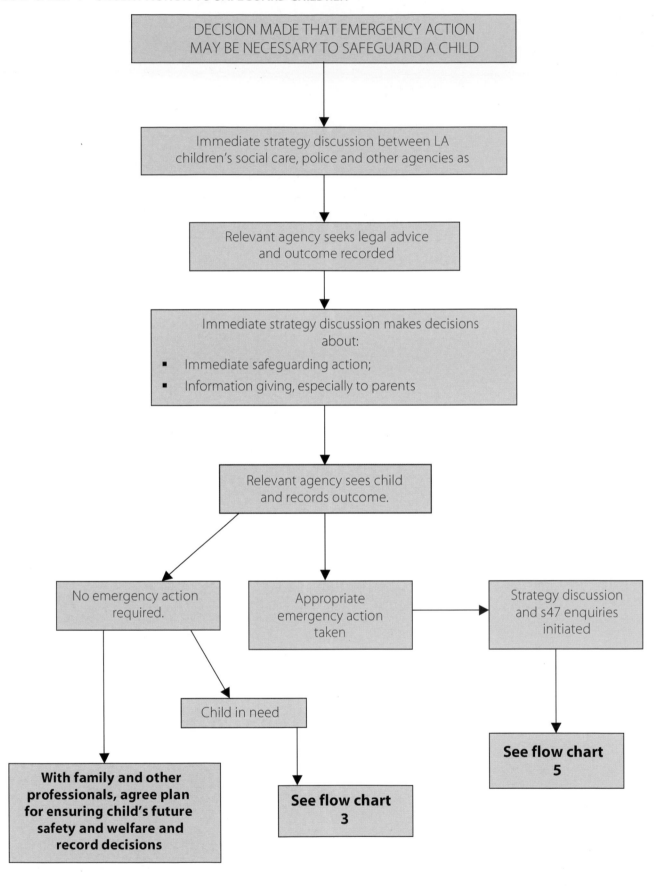

DECISION MADE THAT EMERGENCY ACTION MAY BE NECESSARY TO SAFEGUARD A CHILD

Immediate strategy discussion between LA children's social care, police and other agencies as

Relevant agency seeks legal advice and outcome recorded

Immediate strategy discussion makes decisions about:
- Immediate safeguarding action;
- Information giving, especially to parents

Relevant agency sees child and records outcome.

No emergency action required.

Appropriate emergency action taken

Strategy discussion and s47 enquiries initiated

Child in need

With family and other professionals, agree plan for ensuring child's future safety and welfare and record decisions

See flow chart 3

See flow chart 5

FLOW CHART 5 – WHAT HAPPENS AFTER THE STRATEGY DISCUSSION?

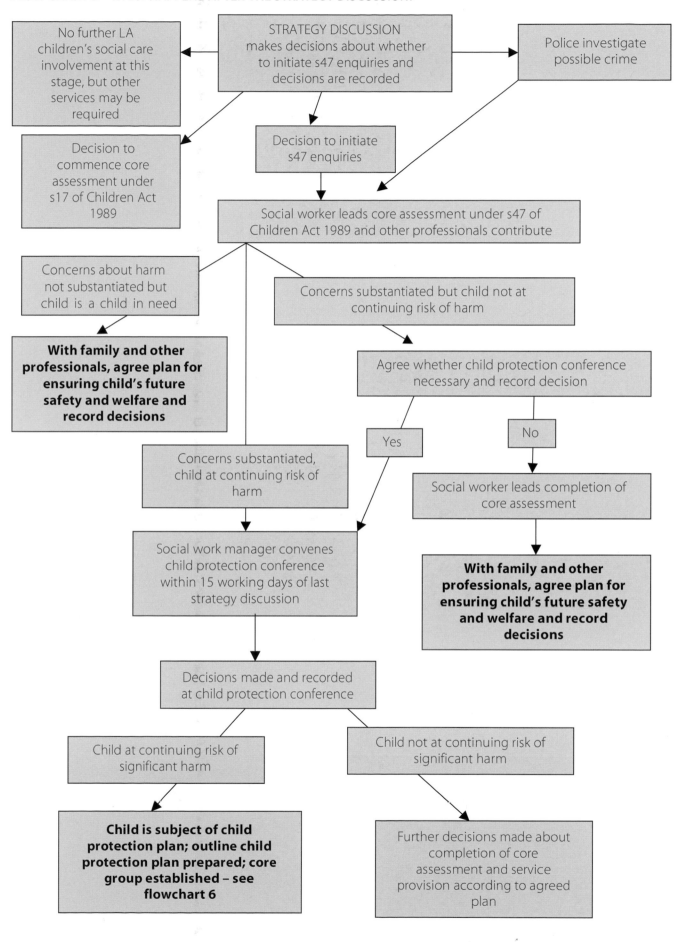

No further LA children's social care involvement at this stage, but other services may be required

STRATEGY DISCUSSION makes decisions about whether to initiate s47 enquiries and decisions are recorded

Police investigate possible crime

Decision to commence core assessment under s17 of Children Act 1989

Decision to initiate s47 enquiries

Social worker leads core assessment under s47 of Children Act 1989 and other professionals contribute

Concerns about harm not substantiated but child is a child in need

Concerns substantiated but child not at continuing risk of harm

With family and other professionals, agree plan for ensuring child's future safety and welfare and record decisions

Agree whether child protection conference necessary and record decision

Yes

No

Concerns substantiated, child at continuing risk of harm

Social worker leads completion of core assessment

Social work manager convenes child protection conference within 15 working days of last strategy discussion

With family and other professionals, agree plan for ensuring child's future safety and welfare and record decisions

Decisions made and recorded at child protection conference

Child at continuing risk of significant harm

Child not at continuing risk of significant harm

Child is subject of child protection plan; outline child protection plan prepared; core group established – see flowchart 6

Further decisions made about completion of core assessment and service provision according to agreed plan

FLOW CHART 6 – WHAT HAPPENS AFTER THE CHILD PROTECTION CONFERENCE, INCLUDING THE REVIEW PROCESS?

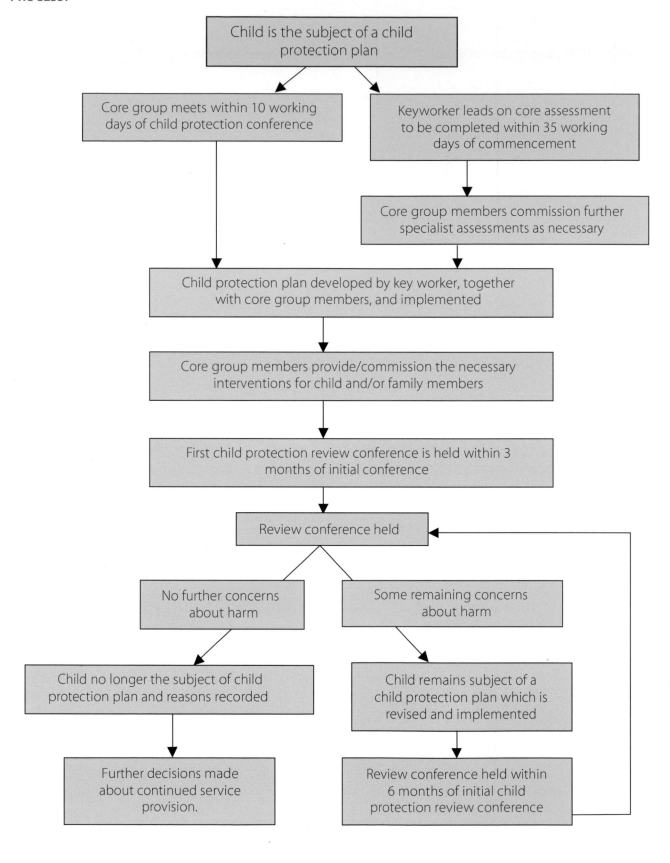

Chapter Five
Roles and responsibilities of the Local Safeguarding Children Board

5.1 The roles and responsibilities of Local Safeguarding Children Boards (LSCBs) are set out fully in Chapter 3 of *Working Together*.

5.2 The LSCB is the key statutory mechanism for agreeing how the relevant organisations in each local area will co-operate to safeguard and promote the welfare of children in that locality, and for ensuring the effectiveness of what they do.

5.3 The LSCB should be chaired by a person of sufficient standing and expertise to command the respect and support of all partners. The Chair should act objectively and distinguish their role as LSCB Chair from any day to day role.

5.4 The LSCB must include representatives of the LA and its Board partners, the statutory organisations that are required to co-operate with the LA in the establishment and operation of the Board and have shared responsibility for the effective discharge of its functions. These are the Board partners set out in section 13(3) of the Children Act (2004):

- district councils in local government areas that have them;
- the chief police officer for a police area of which any part falls within the area of the LA;
- the local probation board for an area of which any part falls within the area of the LA;
- the Youth Offending Team for an area of which any part falls within the area of the LA;
- Strategic Health Authorities and Primary Care Trusts for an area of which any part falls within the area of the LA;
- NHS Trusts and NHS Foundation Trusts, all or most of whose hospitals or establishments and facilities are situated in the LA area;
- the Connexions service operating in any part of the area of the LA;
- CAFCASS (Children and Family Courts Advisory and Support Service);
- the Governor or Director of any Secure Training Centre in the area of the LA; and
- the Governor or Director of any prison in the LA area that ordinarily detains children.

5.5 The LA should also secure the involvement of other relevant local organisations and of the NSPCC where a representative is made available. The LSCB should make appropriate arrangements at a strategic management level to involve others in its work as needed. For example, there may be some organisations or individuals that are, in theory, represented by the statutory Board partners, but that need to be engaged because of their particular role in service provision to children and families, or their role in public protection.

5.6 Each LSCB will have in place local procedures for safeguarding and promoting the welfare of children. These will include guidance on thresholds for referring children who may be in need to LA children's social care, the conduct of section 47 enquiries and associated police investigations; child protection conferences; and deciding whether a child should be the subject of a child protection plan. These procedures will also apply to the management of cases involving fabricated or induced illness, but should be read in conjunction with this guidance. It is not intended that LSCBs have separate guidance on fabricated or induced illness in children, but that local safeguarding children board procedures should reflect this guidance.

Designated and named health professionals

5.7 Each PCT is responsible for ensuring it has a designated doctor and designated nurse to take a strategic, professional lead on all aspects of the health service contribution to safeguarding children across the PCT area, which includes all providers. PCTs should ensure establishment levels of designated and named professionals are proportionate to the local resident populations, following any mergers, and to the complexity of provider arrangements. For large PCTs, NHS Trusts and Foundation Trusts that may have a number of sites, a team approach can enhance the ability to provide 24-hour advice and provide mutual support for those carrying out the designated and named professional role. If this approach is taken, it is important to ensure that the leadership and accountability arrangements are clear. These designated health professionals are a vital source of professional advice on matters relating to safeguarding for other professionals, the PCT, LA Children's Services and the LSCB.

5.8 All NHS Trusts, NHS Foundation Trusts & PCTs providing services for children should identify a named doctor and a named nurse/midwife for safeguarding children. Each NHS Direct site, Ambulance Trust and independent provider should have a named professional for child protection. The named doctor and named nurse will take a professional lead on safeguarding children matters within their own organisations.

Specific responsibilities of an LSCB

5.9 The specific responsibilities of an LSCB in relation to cases involving fabricated or induced illness are:

- to ensure that the LSCB safeguarding children procedures reflect this guidance;
- to ensure that there is a level of agreement and understanding across agencies about operational definitions and thresholds for referral and intervention, and to communicate

clearly to individual services and professional groups their shared responsibility for protecting children within the framework of this national guidance;

- to encourage and help develop effective working relationships between different services and professional groups, based on trust and mutual understanding;

- to audit and evaluate how well local services work together to safeguard children, to improve joint working in the light of knowledge gained through national and local experience and research, and to make sure that any lessons learned are shared, understood, and acted upon;

- to identify the number of children in need who are at risk of significant harm as a result of fabricated or induced illness, or who have suffered significant harm, and to identify resource gaps (in terms of funding and/or the contribution of different agencies);

- to help improve the quality of work to safeguard and promote the welfare of children who have illness induced or fabricated by specifying the training needs of practitioners and managers, and to ensuring that this training is delivered; and

- to raise awareness within the wider community of the need to safeguard children who may be at risk of this type of abuse and promote their welfare, and to explain how the wider community can contribute to these objectives.

5.10 Where the LSCB has a planned programme of work on fabricated or induced illness, this should be agreed and endorsed by all the Board members within the framework of the Children's and Young People's plan, and should be set out in its own plan. The LSCB may find it useful to set up a working group or sub-group, on a short-term or a standing basis, to carry out specific tasks and/or to provide specialist advice in relation to this guidance.

Chapter Six
Working with children and families: key issues

Introduction

6.1 Common principles and ways of working which should underpin the practice of all agencies and professionals working to safeguard children and promote their welfare are set out in Chapter 10 of *Working Together*. This chapter describes how these principles might be used when working with families where illness is being fabricated or induced in a child.

6.2 Family members have a unique role and importance in the lives of children, and children attach great value to their family relationships. Family members know more about their family than any professional could possibly know and well-founded decisions about a child should draw upon this knowledge and understanding. Family members should normally have the right to know what is being said about them, and to contribute to important decisions about their lives and those of their children. Research findings brought together in *Child Protection: Messages from Research* (Department of Health, 1995) and the *Children Act Now: Messages from Research* (Department of Health, 2001) endorse the importance of good relationships between professionals and families in helping to bring about the best possible outcomes for children.

What is meant by working with children and families when safeguarding children?

6.3 Where there are concerns about significant harm to a child, children's social care have a statutory duty to make enquiries and if necessary, statutory powers to intervene to safeguard and promote the child's welfare. Where there is compulsory intervention in family life in this way, parents should still be helped and encouraged to play as large a part as possible in decisions about their child. Children of sufficient age and understanding should be kept fully informed of processes involving them, should be consulted sensitively, and decisions about their future should take account of their wishes and feelings.

6.4 Principles underpinning work to safeguard and promote the welfare of children are set in paragraph 5.4 of *Working Together*. One of these principles is to involve children and families such that children are listened to and their wishes and feelings understood as well and working with parents or colleagues so that they feel respected and informed about what is happening.

6.5 Partnership does **not** mean always agreeing with parents or other adult family members, or always seeking a way forward which is acceptable to them. The aim of safeguarding children processes is to **ensure the safety and welfare of the child, and the child's interests should always be paramount**. Not all parents may be able to safeguard their children's welfare, even with help and support. Some children may be vulnerable to manipulation by a perpetrator of abuse. A minority of parents are actively dangerous to their children, other family members, or professionals, and unwilling and/or unable to change. A clear focus on the child's safety and what is best for the child should always be maintained.

Working with children and families

6.6   Those working together to safeguard children should agree a common understanding in each case, and at each stage of work, of how children and families will be involved in safeguarding children processes, and what information is shared with them. There should be a presumption of openness, joint decision making, and a willingness to listen to families and capitalise on their strengths, but the guiding principle should always be what is in the best interests of the child.

6.7   Where it is suspected or confirmed that illness has been fabricated or induced in a child, all decisions about what and when to tell parents and children should be taken by senior staff within the multi-agency team. While professionals should seek, in general, to discuss any concerns with the family and, where possible, seek their agreement to action, **this should only be done where such discussion and agreement-seeking will not place a child at increased risk of significant harm**. In all cases where the police are involved, the decision about when to inform the parents (about referrals from third parties) will have a bearing on the conduct of police investigation (see paragraph 5.20 of *Working Together*).

6.8   Some information known to professionals will be treated confidentially and should not be automatically shared in front of some children or some adult family members. Such information might include personal health information about particular family members, unless consent has been given, or information which, if disclosed, could compromise criminal investigations or proceedings.

6.9   Agencies and professionals should be honest and explicit with children and families about professional roles, responsibilities, powers and expectations, and about what is and is not negotiable.

6.10   Working relationships with families should develop according to individual circumstances. From the outset, professionals should assess if, when and how the involvement of different family members – both children and adults – can contribute to safeguarding and promoting the welfare of a particular child or group of children. This assessment may change over time as more information becomes available or as families feel supported by professionals. Professional supervision and peer group discussions are important in helping to explore knowledge and perceptions of families' strengths and weaknesses and the safety and welfare of the child within the family, and how family members can play a role in the future safety of the child.

6.11 Family structures are increasingly complex. In addition to those adults who have daily care of a child, estranged parents (for example, birth fathers), grandparents or other family members may play a significant part in the child's life, and some may have parental responsibility even if they are not involved in day to day care. Some children may have been supported during family difficulties by adults from outside the family. Professionals should make sure that they pay attention to the views of all those who have something significant to contribute to decisions about the child's future. Children can provide valuable help in identifying adults they see as important supportive influences in their lives. It is equally important to identify any adult family members who may knowingly or unknowingly support the abusive parent in ways which mean the child is continuing to be abused. The nature of all family relationships should be taken account of when planning placements outside the birth family and contact between the child and the abusing parent.

Involving children

6.12 Research has shown that over 50% of children in whom illness is fabricated or induced are aged under 5 years. This means a significant proportion of children about whom there are concerns are unlikely to be able to be directly involved in discussions about the nature of their abuse. For these young children, it will be important to gain information by observing the child's interactions with family members, peers and professional staff and noticing any differences between the child's interactions with different people, as well as listening carefully to the child. For children who use specific communication methods, it is important that they are enabled to communicate using their normal means of communication. This may require the involvement of a specialist with knowledge of their means of communication (see paragraphs 3.128 – 3.138 in the Assessment Framework Practice Guidance (Department of Health, 2000a) and materials referenced on the ICS website: www.ecm.gov.uk/ics.

6.13 Listening to children and hearing their messages requires training and special skills, including the ability to win their trust and promote a sense of safety. Most children feel loyalty towards those who care for them, and have difficulty saying anything against them. Many do not wish to share confidences, or may not have the language or concepts to describe what has happened to them. Some may fear reprisals, or their removal from home and loss of siblings.

6.14 Children of sufficient age and understanding often have a clear perception of what needs to be done to ensure their safety and wellbeing. Some older children may be very aware of, for example, being given unprescribed substances by a parent or being encouraged to fabricate different types of illness behaviour. Whilst all children will want this abusive behaviour to stop, some may knowingly choose to co-operate with their parents' wishes in order to maintain current family relationships but remain clear in their own minds that they are well. Other children, as a result of the way in which their parent has taught them to behave as if they are ill, may not be able to distinguish between reality and fabrication. These children seem to come to believe their symptoms are real and this false perception of being ill is reinforced and rewarded by their abusing parent.

6.15 If children have had illness fabricated or induced, professionals will need to decide when and how to involve them in the decision-making and planning processes. These decisions should be taken as part of the overall plan for therapeutic work with the family and take account of the fragile family relationships which have enabled the child to have been abused. According to their age and understanding, children should know how safeguarding children processes work, how they can be involved, and that they can contribute to decisions about their future. However, they should understand that ultimately, decisions will be taken in the light of all the available information contributed by themselves, professionals, their parents and other family members, and other significant adults.

Support, advice and advocacy to children and families

6.16 However sensitively enquiries are handled, many families perceive as painful and intrusive professional involvement in their lives which they have not requested, particularly if they feel that their care of their children is being called into question. This should always be acknowledged. Agencies and professionals can do a considerable amount to make safeguarding processes less stressful for families by adopting the principles set out above. Families will also feel better supported if it is clear that interventions in their lives, while firmly focused on the safety and welfare of the child, are concerned also with the wider needs of the child and family.

6.17 Children and families may be supported through their involvement in safeguarding children processes by advice and advocacy services, and they should always be informed of those services which exist locally and nationally. Independent Advocates provide independent and confidential information, advice, representation and support, and can play a vital role in the ensuring children have appropriate information and support to communicate their views in formal settings, such as child protection conferences and court proceedings.

6.18 Where children and families are involved as witnesses in criminal proceedings, the police, witness support services and other services such as those provided by Victim Support, can do a great deal to explain the process, make it feel less daunting and ensure that children are prepared for and supported in the court process. The practice guidance *Provision of Therapy for Child Witnesses prior to a Criminal Trial* (2001) makes it clear that the bests interest of a child are paramount when deciding whether, and in what form, therapeutic help is given to child witnesses. Information about the Criminal Injuries Compensation Scheme should also be provided in relevant cases.

Information sharing

6.19 Sharing of information in cases of concern about children's welfare enables professionals to consider jointly how to proceed in the best interests of the child and to safeguard children more generally.

6.20 In dealing with alleged offences involving a child victim, the police should normally work in partnership with children's social care and/or other agencies. While the responsibility to instigate a criminal investigation rests with the police, they should consider the views expressed by other agencies. There will be less serious cases where, after discussion, it is agreed that the best interests of the child are served by a children's social care led intervention rather than a full police investigation.

6.21 In deciding whether there is a need to share information, professionals should consider their legal obligations, including whether they have a duty of confidentiality to the child. Where there is such a duty, the professional may lawfully share information if a competent child (or the parent of a child who lacks competence) consents or if there is a public interest of sufficient force. This must be judged by the professional on the facts of each case. Where there is a clear risk of significant harm to a child, or serious harm to adults, the public interest test will almost certainly be satisfied. However, there will be other cases where practitioners will be justified in sharing some confidential information in order to make decisions on sharing further information or taking action – the information shared should be proportionate.

6.22 The child's best interests must be the overriding consideration in making decisions about sharing information. The cross-Government practice guidance, *Information sharing: Practitioners' guide* (HM Government, 2006b), provides advice on these issues – see www.everychildmatters.gov.uk. Any decision on whether or not to share information must be properly documented. Decisions in this area need to be made by, or with the advice of, people with suitable competence in child protection work, such as named or designated professionals or senior managers.

The Data Protection Act

6.23 The Data Protection Act 1998 requires that personal information is obtained and processed fairly and lawfully; only disclosed in appropriate circumstances; is accurate, relevant and not held longer than necessary; and is kept securely. Where information is not held under any duty of confidentiality the Act allows for disclosure without the consent of the subject in certain conditions, including for the purposes of the prevention or detection of crime, or the apprehension or prosecution of offenders, and where failure to disclose would be likely to prejudice those objectives in a particular case (for further guidance see *Data Protection Act 1998: protection and use of patient information* (Department of Health, 1998). Legal advice should be sought where appropriate or in cases of doubt.

Record keeping

6.24 The recording and retention of information, including information about covert video surveillance, should be made in accordance with the Data Protection Act 1998. In particular bodies need to be mindful of the eight Data Protection Principles – for example the requirement that the information is adequate, relevant and not excessive in relation to the purpose or purposes for which it is held (principle 3); it is accurate and up to date (principle 4); it is not kept for any longer than it is necessary to do so (principle 5) and appropriate technical and organisational measures are taken to guard against unlawful or unauthorised processing or accidental loss or destruction of or damage to the information (principle 7).

6.25 Good record keeping is an important part of the accountability of professionals to those who use their services. It helps to focus work, and is essential to support effective working across agency and professional boundaries. Clear and accurate records ensure that there is a documented account of an agency, or professional's involvement with a child and/or family. They help with continuity when individual workers are unavailable, or change, and they provide an essential tool for managers to monitor work or for audit and peer review. Records are an essential source of evidence for section 47 enquiries, and may also be required to be disclosed in court proceedings. Records relating to cases where enquiries do not result in the substantiation of referral concerns should be retained in accordance with individual agency record retention policies. These policies should ensure that records are stored securely and can be retrieved promptly and efficiently. Health records should be kept in accordance with the *Records Management: NHS Code of Practice* (Department of Health, 2006).

6.26 To serve these purposes, records should use clear, straightforward language, should be concise, and should be accurate not only in fact, but also in differentiating between opinion, judgements and hypothesis. Where it is considered that illness may be being fabricated or induced, the records relating to the child's symptoms, illnesses, diagnosis and treatments should always include the name (and agency) of the person who gave or reported the information, and be dated and signed legibly. All telephone conversations should be recorded fully.

6.27 All records should be kept securely to prevent unauthorised access and ensure they cannot be interfered with.

6.28 Well kept records provide an essential underpinning to good safeguarding children practice, and are particularly important in cases where it is suspected that illness is being fabricated or induced in a child. They are equally important when abuse is substantiated. Information should be brought together from a number of sources, and their veracity and accuracy checked before making careful professional judgements on the basis of this information. Records should be clear and comprehensive, and judgements made, and action and decisions taken should be carefully recorded. Health records, in particular, should record accurately all investigations, results, observations and consent to undertake examinations or treatment. Doctors should follow the principles of record keeping set out in the General Medical Council's *Good Medical Practice* (GMC, 2006). Documents should include photographic evidence and good diagrams depicting the site of any injuries along with measurements. Nurses and midwives should follow the principles of good record keeping set out in the Nursing & Midwifery Council's *Advice on Record Keeping* (NMC, 2006). Where decisions have been taken jointly across agencies, or endorsed by a manager, this should be clearly recorded. All decisions to undertake covert video surveillance should be recorded in the child's records held by each agency involved in the decision and signed by a senior manager.

6.29 Where a child has been referred to children's social care, information about the referral and subsequent work undertaken with child and family must be recorded (see www.ecm.gov.uk/ics).

These records should include a detailed chronology of the case. Specifically, the reader should be able to track:

- the relevant history of the child and family which led to any statutory intervention;

- the nature of these interventions, including planned outcomes;

- the means by which change is to be achieved; *and*

- the progress which is being made in achieving these outcomes.

6.30 The recording of a detailed chronology which includes the medical, psychiatric and social histories of the child, parents, siblings and other significant family members is particularly important when identifying fabricated or induced illness in a child. It enables patterns of presentation for medical treatment to be recognised not only for the child but also across generational boundaries. It will also inform decisions about how best to provide the services necessary to safeguard the child's welfare and achieve change in the family.

6.31 Careful consideration should be given to which agencies and professionals need to be informed about relevant changes of circumstances, for example the change of GP of a child who is the subject of a child protection plan. Each agency should ensure that when a child moves from their area, the child's records are transferred promptly to the relevant agency within the new locality. A telephone discussion followed up by a written summary may be necessary pending transfer of the records to ensure continuity of safe care. Where children have had illness fabricated or induced, it is essential that the new professionals involved are fully aware of the child's history to enable them to continue to monitor appropriately the child's health and development. Many families use NHS Direct who are able to flag when a child has a child protection plan if they are informed of this information.

6.32 Requests for access to the child's records should be actioned in accordance with each agency's Access to Records policy and procedures. Where a child is not Gillick competent and a parent seeks access to his medical notes, access to all or part of the notes can be denied where disclosing the information would, in the view of an appropriate health professional, be likely to cause serious harm to the physical or mental health or condition of the child or any other person (see the Data Protection (Subject Access Modification) (Health) Order 2000 SI No 413). Access should also be denied if the child explicitly or implicitly makes it clear that they would not want information to be disclosed to their parents (Reg 5(3) and (4) of SI No 413).

6.33 A health professional is defined in section 69 of the Data Protection Act 1998 and includes a registered medical practitioner, a registered nurse or midwife, a clinical psychologist, child psychotherapist or speech and language therapist. An appropriate health professional is broadly the health professional who has the most recent and relevant care of the child.

6.34 Where there is any doubt about the retention or disclosure of information, legal advice should be sought.

Use of covert video surveillance

6.35 The use of covert video surveillance (CVS) is governed by the Regulation of Investigatory Powers Act 2000 (the 2000 Act). After a decision has been made at a multi-agency strategy discussion to use CVS in a case of suspected fabricated or induced illness, **the surveillance should be undertaken by the police**. The operation should be controlled by the police and accountability for it held by a police manager. The police should supply and install any equipment, and be responsible for the security of and archiving of the video tapes.

6.36 **CVS should be used if there is no alternative way of obtaining information which will explain the child's signs and symptoms, and the multi-agency strategy discussion meeting considers that its use is justified based on the medical information available** (see also paragraph 5.7 of *Fabricated or Induced Illness by Carers* (Royal College of Paediatrics and Child Health, 2002)). The police will only be able to carry out CVS if they obtain the necessary authorisation under the 2000 Act. In summary, this means that they will need to demonstrate that the use of CVS is necessary to detect or prevent crime or serious crime within the meaning of the 2000 Act, depending on the type of surveillance intended, and that the evidence cannot be gathered by other less intrusive means. It is, therefore, likely to be used in a minority of cases. It is important that only those who need to know CVS is being used are involved in discussions and planning about its use. When it has been decided to use CVS the LSCB safeguarding children procedures should be followed. Police officers should carry out any necessary monitoring, and all personnel, including nursing staff, who will be involved in its use should have received specialist training in this area.

6.37 The consultant paediatrician responsible for the child's care should ensure that the necessary medical and nursing staff are available to support the police during this operation. Their role will be to provide the child with immediate and appropriate health care when necessary. The level and nature of health involvement during the period of covert video surveillance should be agreed at the strategy discussion and all relevant staff briefed on the arrangements for the child's health care.

6.38 The safety (both short and long-term) and health of the child is the over-riding factor in the planning and carrying out of covert video surveillance. The primary aim of undertaking covert video surveillance is to identify whether the child is having illness induced, in situations where a multi-agency decision has been taken, at a strategy discussion, that its use is justified (see paragraph 4.29). Of secondary importance is the obtaining of criminal evidence. In any event, the use of CVS must be proportionate to the aim to be achieved. Legal advice should be sought where appropriate, or in cases of doubt.

6.39 Children's social care should have a contingency plan in place which can be implemented immediately if CVS provides evidence that the child is being harmed.

6.40 Plans should also take account of the possibility that there may be no evidence of abuse, but the child may be a child in need.

Allegations against Staff

6.41 Experience has shown that children can be subjected to abuse by those who work with them in any and all settings. Allegations may arise from a range of sources, including children themselves, parents, staff, foster carers or volunteers. Regardless of the source of the concern, allegations should be taken seriously and treated with accordance with Appendix 5 in *Working Together* (2006) and Chapter 5 of *Safeguarding Children and Safer Recruitment in Education* (2006).

6.42 In this area of work, it is also the case that concerns may be expressed by parents/carers about one or more members of medical, nursing or other staff who are responsible for medical investigation, diagnosis or treatment of their child. Such concerns may or may not include elements of alleged abuse by the member of staff against the subject child. Similarly, such expressions of concerns may not relate to allegations of actual abusive behaviour by staff, but instead, in effect, be complaints which should be dealt with in accordance with the relevant agency's complaints handling process (see paragraph 6.61).

6.43 If there is cause to suspect a child is suffering, or is likely to suffer, significant harm, a strategy discussion should be convened in accordance with paragraph 5.54 of *Working Together*. In these cases the strategy discussion should include a representative of the employer (unless there are good reasons not to do that) and should take account of any information the employer can provide about the circumstances or context of the allegations.

6.44 In the case of unexpected death or serious untoward harm in hospital, the NHS should also follow the *Memorandum of Understanding and Guidelines for the NHS (2006)*.

6.45 There may be up to three strands in the consideration of allegations:

- Police investigation into a possible criminal offence;

- Enquiries and assessment by children's social care about whether a child is in need of protection or in need of services; and

- Consideration by an employer of disciplinary action in respect of the individual.

6.46 It is important that employers keep a clear and comprehensive summary of any allegations made, details of how the allegations were followed up and resolved, and of any action taken and decisions reached. These should be kept in a person's confidential personnel file and a copy should be given to the individual. Such information should be retained on file, including for people who leave the organisation, at least until the person reaches normal retirement age, or for 10 years if that is longer. The purpose of the record is to enable accurate information to be given in response to any future request for a reference. It will provide clarification in cases where a future CRB Disclosure reveals information from the police that an allegation was made but did not result in a prosecution or a conviction. It will also prevent unnecessary re-investigation if, as sometimes happens, allegations resurface after a period of time (see Working Together, paragraph 9, page 241).

6.47 The possible risk of harm to children posed by an accused person needs to be evaluated and managed effectively – in respect of the child(ren) involved in the allegations, and any other children in the individual's home, work or community life. In some cases this requires the employer to consider suspending the person. Suspension should be considered in any case where there is cause to suspect a child is at risk of significant harm, or the allegation warrants investigation by the police, or is so serious that it might be grounds for dismissal. People must not be suspended automatically or without careful thought. Employers must consider carefully whether the circumstances of a case warrant a person being suspended from contact with children until the allegation is resolved. Note: neither the LA, nor the police, nor children's social care can require an employer to suspend a member of staff or a volunteer. The power to suspend is vested in the employer alone. However, where a strategy discussion or initial evaluation discussion concludes that there should be enquiries by social care and/or an investigation by the police, the LA designated officer should canvass police/social care views about whether the accused member of staff needs to be suspended from contact with children, to inform the employer's consideration of suspension (see Working Together, paragraph 20, page 243).

Effective support and supervision

6.48 Working with children and families where it is suspected or confirmed that illness is being fabricated or induced in a child requires sound professional judgements to be made. It is demanding work that can be distressing and stressful. Practitioners are likely to need support to enable them to deal with the feelings the suspicion or identification of this type of abuse engenders, particularly if they have been very involved in the child's previous care and have formed close relationships with the family. It can be very distressing to a professional person, who has come to know a family well and trusted them, to have to deal with their feelings when they learn a child's illness has been caused by actions of that child's primary carer.

6.49 All of those involved in such work should have access to advice and support, for example, from peers, managers, named and designated professionals and external professionals with experience of fabricated or induced illness. For health professionals, the named doctor or nurse for safeguarding children matters within the Trust or Board will provide advice on how to manage these cases. If unavailable, or for those health professionals working independently, the designated doctor or nurse within the relevant PCT in England or Local Health Board in Wales will fulfil this role. Supervisors should be available to practitioners as an important source of advice and expertise, and may be required to endorse judgements at certain key points in the safeguarding processes. Supervisors should also record key decisions within case records.

6.50 It is not uncommon for staff within a team to have different opinions on how to manage cases where illness is being fabricated or induced in a child. This phenomenon is more likely when some staff do not believe that illness is being fabricated or induced in the child despite the objective evidence. Where these situations arise senior staff should take responsibility for deciding how to manage this conflict. Open discussion of feelings and problems within the staff group can be very helpful. One option may be to use a professional from either within the team or who is well-known to the team, such as a child and family psychiatrist, to assist them in managing this group process: another may be to engage the services of an independent person who has the appropriate skills. Irrespective of the method chosen, it is essential that staff are helped to understand what actions are necessary to safeguard the child's welfare and are clear that they should carry out their role according to the agreed multi-agency plan.

6.51 For many practitioners involved in day-to-day work with children and families, effective supervision is important to promote good standards of practice and to support individual staff members. Supervision should help to ensure that practice is soundly based and consistent with LSCB and organisational procedures. Supervision should help to ensure that practitioners fully understand their roles, responsibilities, and the scope of their professional discretion and authority. It should also help to identify the training and development needs of practitioners, so that each has the skills to provide an effective service. In some instances staff themselves may come under suspicion for fabricating or inducing illness. For health staff this may require them to change their working practice. for example, two nurses undertaking all the child's care so that they cannot be accused of harming the child if suspicions are not substantiated. This situation should be dealt with as set out in paragraphs 6.41-6.47 of this guidance.

Inter-agency training and development

6.52 Chapter 4 in *Working Together* sets out in detail the importance of inter-agency training and development to support the use of the guidance. This section does not repeat what is set out in *Working Together*, but addresses the specific training implications of identifying and managing situations where it is suspected or known that illness is being fabricated or induced in a child by a carer. Training on fabricated or induced illness in children requires specialist knowledge and the training needs of one discipline may be quite different to those of another. This requirement should be built into programme planning, and programmes tailored to address the range of professional roles and responsibilities set out earlier in Chapter 3. To assist employers fulfil their responsibilities for training and continuing professional development, DCSF has commissioned inter-agency training materials *Incredibly Caring* (2008).

6.53 Staff should be able to exercise professional skill in terms of effective information sharing where they have concerns about illness fabrication or induction. They should also be able to use their knowledge and skills in collaborating with other agencies and disciplines in this area of work. They need a sound understanding of the legislative framework within which they will be working, especially with regard to the use of covert video surveillance and information sharing. *Information Sharing: practitioners' guide* (HM Government, 2006b) provides practitioners with guidance on when and how to share information legally.

6.54 Individual agencies are responsible for ensuring that staff are competent and confident in carrying out their responsibilities for safeguarding and promoting children's welfare. Continuing professional development should be supported to enable their employees to develop and maintain the necessary knowledge, values and skills to work together to safeguard and promote the welfare of children.

6.55 Employers should ensure that their employees are aware of how to recognise and respond to safeguarding concerns including the fabrication or induction of illness. This knowledge and expertise should be put in place before employees attend inter-agency training. Employers also have a responsibility to identify adequate resources and support for inter-agency training by:

- providing staff who have the relevant expertise to support the LSCB (e.g. by sitting on an LSCB training sub-group, and/or contributing to training);

- allocating the time required to complete inter-agency training tasks effectively;

- releasing staff to attend the appropriate inter-agency training courses;

- ensuring that staff receive relevant single-agency training that enables them to maximise the learning derived from inter-agency training, and have opportunities to consolidate learning from inter-agency training; and

- contributing to the planning, resourcing, delivery and evaluation of training.

6.56 Local authorities (LAs), with their partners in children's trusts, are responsible for ensuring that workforce strategies are developed in their local area. This includes making sure that training opportunities to meet needs identified by the LSCBs are available. They should establish systems for the delivery of single-agency and inter-agency training on safeguarding and promoting the welfare of children. They should consider, in discussion with the LSCB, which bodies should commission or deliver the training including that on fabricated or induced illness.

6.57 All PCTs and NHS Trusts should ensure appropriate training is available to professional staff at all levels and in all disciplines including surgery. PCTs should also satisfy themselves in their roles as commissioners of services, that appropriate training is available to all those in organisations which have regular contact with children. Named doctors and nurses in conjunction with designated doctors and nurses are responsible for advising on such training. The Royal Colleges have a role in incorporating appropriate training in the recommended syllabuses of both post–graduate and continuing professional development programmes.

The purpose of inter-agency training

6.58 Training should be available at a number of levels to address the learning needs of different staff. The framework set out in *Working Together* (paragraphs 4.20 – 4.22) outlines three stages of training, and matches them with target audiences that have different degrees of involvement or decision-making responsibility for children's welfare. Decisions should be made locally about how the stages are most appropriately delivered in respect of fabricated or induced illness in children and this should be part of the local workforce training strategy developed to meet the needs identified by the LSCB.

6.59 There are significant numbers of people who are in contact with children living away from their families. Their introductory training on safeguarding children should include being alert to children who are deemed to be ill by their parents but who do not exhibit the expected signs and symptoms of such an illness and knowing who to discuss any concerns with in accordance with the LSCB safeguarding children procedures.

6.60 The detailed content of training at each level of the framework shown should be specified locally. The content of training programmes should be regularly reviewed and updated in the light of research and practice experience. *Incredibly Caring* (2008) – a training resource pack to support effective implementation of this guidance – has been designed for delivery to a diverse range of staff including multi-agency or multi-disciplinary audiences, staff attending single agency training courses and those attending team training events. The training materials are intended for delivery to the children's workforce and adult services who come into contact with children and families and work in the statutory, voluntary, and independent sectors.

Complaints procedures

6.61 Complaints about individual agencies, their performance and provision (or non-provision) of services should be responded to in accordance with the relevant agency's complaints handling process. For example, LA children's social care is required (by s26 of the Children Act 1989) to establish complaints procedures to deal with complaints arising in respect of Part III of the Act.

6.62 Parents/caregivers – and, on occasion, children – may have concerns about which they may wish to make representations or complain, in respect of one or more of the following aspects of the functioning of child protection conferences:

- the process of the conference

- the outcome, in terms of the fact of and/or the category of primary concern at the time the child became the subject of a child protection plan

- a decision for the child to become or not to become, the subject of a child protection plan or not to cease the child being the subject of a child protection plan.

6.63 Complaints about aspects of the functioning of conferences described above should be addressed to the conference Chair. Such complaints should be passed on to LA children's social care which should deal with them as if they had been made in relation to functions under Part III of the Children Act 1889. In considering and responding to complaints, the LA should form an inter-agency panel made up of senior representatives from LSCB member agencies. The panel should consider whether the relevant inter-agency protocols and procedures have been observed correctly, and whether the decision that is being complained about follows reasonably from the proper observation of the protocol(s).

6.64 In addition, representations and complaints may be received by individual agencies in respect of services provided (or not provided) as a consequence of assessments and conferences, including those set out in child protection plans. Such concerns should be responded to by the relevant agency in accordance with its own processes for responding to such matters. Where the complaint involves a health professional the involvement of the designated doctor or nurse will be helpful in planning how best to respond.

Appendix 1
Legislative Framework

United Nations Convention on the Rights of the Child

1.1　This guidance reflects the principles contained within the United Nations Convention on the Rights of the Child, ratified by the UK Government in 1991. Specifically:

- Article 3: State parties shall ensure that the best interests of the child shall be a primary consideration when action is taken concerning children;

- Article 9: State parties should ensure that children shall not be separated from their parents unless such separation is necessary in the best interests of the child;

- Article 19: State parties shall take all appropriate measures to protect children from abuse or neglect;

- Article 37: (a) no child shall be subjected to torture or other cruel, inhumane or degrading treatment or punishment. (b) No child shall be deprived of his or her liberty unlawfully or arbitrarily;

- Article 39: all appropriate measures shall be taken to promote the physical and psychological recovery and social reintegration of a child victim of any form of neglect or abuse.

Children Act 1989

1.2　The guidance is particularly informed by the requirements of the Children Act 1989, which provides a comprehensive framework for the care and protection of children.

1.3　The Children Act 1989 places two specific duties on agencies to co-operate in the interests of vulnerable children:

Section 27 provides that a local authority may request help from:

- any local authority;

- any local education authority;

- any local housing authority;

- Special Health Authority, Primary Care Trust or National Health Service trust[3] or NHS foundation trust; *and*

3.　Including those NHS trusts and PCTs re-designated as Care Trusts under Section 45 of the Health and Social Care Act 2001

- any person authorised by the Secretary of State for the purposes of this section.

in exercising the local authority's functions under Part III of the Act. This part of the Act places a duty on local authorities to provide support and services for children in need, including children looked after by the local authority and those in secure accommodation. The authority whose help is requested in these circumstances has a duty to comply with the request, by taking the action specified by the requesting local authority, provided it is compatible with its other duties and functions and does not unduly prejudice the discharge of any of that authority's functions.

Section 47 places a duty on:

- any local authority;

- any local education authority;

- any local housing authority;

- Special Health Authority, Primary Care Trust, National Health Service Trust or NHS foundation trust; *and*

- any person authorised by the Secretary of State for the purposes of that section.

to help a local authority with its enquiries in cases where the authority are informed that a child who lives, or is found, in their area is the subject of an emergency protection order or is in police protection or has contravened a ban imposed by a curfew notice, or the authority has reasonable cause to suspect that a child is suffering, or is likely to suffer, significant harm, unless doing so would be unreasonable in all the circumstances of the case.

The concept of significant harm

1.4 The Children Act 1989 introduced the concept of significant harm as the threshold justifying compulsory intervention in family life in the best interests of the child. A court may only make a care order (committing the child to the care of the local authority) or supervision order (putting the child under the supervision of a social worker, or a probation officer) in respect of a child if it is satisfied that:

- the child is suffering, or is likely to suffer, significant harm; *and*

- that the harm or likelihood of harm is attributable to a lack of adequate parental care or control (s31).

Under s31(9) of the Children Act 1989:

'harm' means ill-treatment or the impairment of health or development (including, for example, impairment suffered from seeing or hearing the ill-treatment of another);

'development' means physical, intellectual, emotional, social or behavioural development;

'health' means physical or mental health; and

'ill-treatment' includes sexual abuse and forms of ill-treatment which are not physical.

Under s31(10) of the Act:

Where the question of whether harm suffered by a child is significant turns on the child's health and development, his health or development shall be compared with that which could reasonably be expected of a similar child.

1.5 There are no absolute criteria on which to rely when judging what constitutes significant harm. Sometimes, a single traumatic event may constitute significant harm, for example a violent assault, intentional suffocation or poisoning. More often, significant harm is a compilation of significant events, both acute and long-standing, which interrupt, change or damage the child's physical, social and psychological development. Long-term physical or emotional abuse can cause impairment to such an extent that it constitutes significant harm. For each child, it is necessary to consider the harm they have suffered in the context of the family's strengths and supports.

1.6 In deciding whether a child has been or is likely to suffer significant harm, it is necessary to consider the information gathered during an assessment under each dimension heading in the Assessment Framework (Department of Health et al, 2000). This includes:

- the nature of harm, in terms of ill-treatment or failure to provide adequate care;

- the impact on the child's health or development;

- the child's development within the context of their family and wider environment;

- any special needs, such as a medical condition, communication difficulty or disability that may affect the child's development and care within the family;

- the capacity of parents to meet adequately the child's needs; and

- the wider family and environmental context.

The child's reactions, his or her perceptions, and wishes and feelings should be ascertained and taken account of according to the child's age and understanding[4].

---

4. Section 53 of the Children Act 2004 amended s17 and s47 of the children Act 1989, so that before determining what, if any, services to provide to a child in need under s17, or action to take with respect to a child under s47, the wishes and feelings of the child should be ascertained as far as is reasonable and given due consideration.

Children Act 2004

1.7 Section 10 requires each local authority (LA)[5] to make arrangements to promote co-operation between the authority, each of the authority's relevant partners and such other persons or bodies working with children in the LA area as the authority considers appropriate. The arrangements are to be made with a view to improving the wellbeing of children in the authority's area – which includes protection from harm or neglect alongside other adverse outcomes. This section of the Children Act 2004 is the legislative basis for children's trust arrangements.

1.8 Section 11 requires a range of organisations to make arrangements for ensuring that their functions, and services provided on their behalf to discharge those functions, are provided with regard to the need to safeguard and promote the welfare of children.

1.9 Section 12 enables the Secretary of State to require LAs to establish and operate databases relating to the s10 or s11 duties (above) or the section 175 duty (below), or to establish and operate databases nationally. Section 12(4) limits the information that may be included in those databases. Section 11(7) sets out which organisations can be required to, and section 11(8) sets out which organisations can be enabled to, disclose information to be included in the databases.

1.10 Section 13 requires each children's services authority to establish an LSCB. It also requires a range of organisations to take part in LSCBs. Sections 13–16 set out the framework for LSCBs, and the LSCB Regulations set out the requirements in more detail, in particular on LSCB functions.

Education Act 2002

1.11 Section 175 puts a duty on local education authorities (in its capacity as a local education authority), maintained (state) schools and further education institutions, including sixth-form colleges, to ensure that their functions conferred on them in a particular capacity are exercised with a view to safeguarding and promoting the welfare of children – children who are pupils, and students under 18 years in the case of schools and colleges.

1.12 The same duty is put on independent schools, including academies, by The Education (Independent Schools Standards) (England) Regulations 2003 made under section 157 of that Act.

Human Rights Act 1998

1.13 The Human Rights Act 1998 is also fundamental to this guidance. Section 6(1) places a duty on all public authorities to act in a way that is compatible with the rights and freedoms of the European Convention of Human Rights that have been incorporated by the 1998 Act. These convention rights include Article 3 "no one shall be subjected to torture or to inhuman or degrading treatment or punishment" and Article 8 "everyone has the right to respect for his private and family life, his home and his correspondence".

---

5. In this guidance this generally means Local Authorities that are Children's Services Authorities – effectively, local authorities that are responsible for social services and education. Section 63 of the Children Act 2004 defines a Children's Services Authority in England as: a county council in England; a metropolitan district council; a non-metropolitan district council for an area where there is no county council; a London borough council; the Common Council of the City of London and the Council of the Isles of Scilly.

1.14 The Human Rights Act 1998 has been interpreted as placing obligations on public authorities both to refrain from certain action and in some circumstances to take positive steps or measures to protect the Convention rights of individuals.

1.15 A public authority includes "any person certain of whose functions are functions of a public nature". There will be some bodies, for example, local authorities which are clearly public authorities under the Act. However other bodies may exercise both public and private functions and where those functions are of a public nature they must be exercised compatibly with the convention rights incorporated by the Human Rights Act. Where there is any doubt, it is important that bodies seek their own legal advice.

The European Convention on Human Rights

1.16 Article 8 of the European Convention on Human Rights states that:

(1) Everyone has the right to respect for his private and family life, his home and his correspondence.

(2) There shall be no interference by a public authority with the exercise of this right except such as in accordance with the law and is necessary in a democratic society in the interests of national security, public safety or the economic well-being of the country, for the prevention of disorder or crime, for the protection of health or morals, or for the protection of the rights and freedoms of others.

1.17 Disclosure of information without the consent of the data subject or a person acting on their behalf might give rise to an issue under Article 8. Disclosure of information to safeguard children will usually be for the protection of health or morals, for the protection of the rights and freedoms of others, and for the prevention of disorder or crime. Disclosure should be appropriate for the purpose and only to the extent necessary to achieve that purpose. Legal advice should be sought where appropriate, or in cases of doubt.

Regulation of Investigatory Powers Act 2000

1.18 Of particular significance is the Regulation of Investigatory Powers Act 2000. The main purpose of this Act is to ensure that investigatory powers are used in accordance with human rights. These powers include the use of covert surveillance such as covert video surveillance, in the course of specific operations. Part II and Schedule 1 to the Act set out a system of authorisations for the use of surveillance.

References

Adshead G and Brooke D (2001) *Munchausen Syndrome By Proxy. Current Issues in Assessment, Treatment and Research*. Imperial College Press, London.

Bass C and Adshead G (2007) *Fabrication and induction of illness in children: the psychopathology of abuse. Advances in Psychiatric Treatment*. **13**: 169-177.

Berg B and Jones D P H (1999) Outcome of psychiatric intervention in factitious illness by proxy (Munchausen syndrome by proxy). *Archives of Disease in Childhood*. **81**: 0-7.

Black D and Hollis P (1996) Psychiatric treatment of factitious illness in an infant (Munchausen by Proxy Syndrome). *Clinical Child Psychology and Psychiatry*. **1**: 89-98.

Bluglass K (2001) *Treatment of Perpetrators*. In Adshead G and Brooke D (eds) (2001) *Munchausen Syndrome By Proxy. Current Issues in Assessment, Treatment and Research*. Imperial College Press, London.

Bools C N (1996) Factitious Illness by Proxy: Munchausen Syndrome by Proxy. *British Journal of Psychiatry*. ***169****: 268-275.*

Bools C N, Neale B A and Meadow S R (1992) Co-morbidity associated with fabricated illness (Munchausen Syndrome by Proxy). *Archives of Disease in Childhood*. **67**: 77-79.

Bools C N, Neale B A and Meadow S R (1993) Follow up of victims of fabricated illness (Munchausen Syndrome by Proxy). *Archives of Disease in Childhood*. **69**: 625-630.

Bools C N, Neale B A and Meadow S R (1994) Munchausen Syndrome by Proxy: A Study of Psychopathology. *Child Abuse and Neglect*. **18**: 773-788.

Brooke D and Adshead (2001). *Current Challenges in the Management of Perpetrators*. In Adshead G and Brooke D (2001) *Munchausen Syndrome By Proxy. Current Issues in Assessment, Treatment and Research*. Imperial College Press, London

Children Act 1989 (1989). HMSO, London.

Children Act 2004 (2004). HMSO, London.

Cleaver H (2000) *Fostering Family Contact: a study of children, parents and foster carers*. The Stationery Office, London.

Coombe P (1995) The in-patient psychotherapy of a mother and child at the Cassel Hospital: A case of Munchausen's Syndrome by Proxy. *British Journal of Psychotherapy*. **12**: 195-207.

Criminal Justice System (2007) Achieving Best Evidence in Criminal Proceedings: Victims and Witnesses and Using Special Measures. Criminal Justice System, London.

Crown Prosecution Service, Department of Health and Home Office (2001) Provision of Therapy for Child Witnesses prior to a Criminal Trial. Practice Guidance, London CPS. www.cps.gov.uk/publications/docs/therapychild.pdf

Data Protection Act 1998 (1998). HMSO, London.

Davis P, McClure R J, Rolfe K, Chessman N, Pearson S, Sibert J R, Meadow R (1998) Procedures, placement, and risks of further abuse after Munchausen syndrome by proxy, non-accidental poisoning, and non-accidental suffocation. *Archives of Disease in Childhood*. **78(3)**: 217-221.

Department for Children, Schools and Families and the Department of Health (2007) *Statement on the Duties of Doctors and other Health Professionals in Investigations of Child Abuse* (http://www.ecm.gov.uk/resources-and-practice/IG00251/)

Department for Children, Schools and Families (2008) *Incredibly Caring*. Radcliffe Medical Press. Abingdon.

Department for Education and Employment (1999) *School Inclusion: Pupil Support. The Secretary of State's guidance on pupil attendance, behaviour, exclusion and re-integration. Circular No. 10/99*.

Department for Education and Skills (2006) *Safeguarding Children and Safer Recruitment in Education*. Department for Education and Skills, London.

Department for Education and Skills and Department of Health (2005) *Mandatory Medicines*. Department for Education and Skills, London.

Department of Health, Department for Education and Employment and the Home Office (2000) *Framework for the Assessment of Children in Need and their Families*. The Stationery Office, London.

Department of Health (1995) Child Protection: Messages from Research. HMSO, London.

Department of Health (1998) *Data Protection Act 1998: protection and use of patient information*. Department of Health, London.

Department of Health (2000a) *Assessing Children in Need and their Families; Practice Guidance*. The Stationery Office, London.

Department of Health (2000b) *Report of a review of the research framework in North Staffordshire Hospital NHS Trust*. Department of Health, London.

Department of Health (2001) *Children Act Now: Messages from Research*. The Stationery Office, London.

Department of Health (2006) *Memorandum of Understanding , Investigating patient safety incidents involving unexpected death or serious untoward harm: a protocol for liaison and effective communications between the NHS, Association of Chief Police Officers and Health and Safety Executive.* Department of Health, London.

Department of Health (2006) *Guidelines for the NHS in support of the Memorandum of Understanding Investigating patient safety incidents involving unexpected death or serious untoward harm: a protocol for liaison and effective communications between the NHS, Association of Chief Police Officers and Health and Safety Executive.* Department of Health, London.

Department of Health (2006) *Records Management: NHS Code of Practice.* Department of Health, London.

Eminson M (2000a) *Munchausen Syndrome by Proxy Abuse: an introduction.* In Eminson M and Postlethwaite R (2000) *Munchausen Syndrome by Proxy Abuse: A Practice Approach.* Butterworth – Heinemann, Oxford.

Eminson M (2000b) Background In Eminson M and Postlethwaite R (2000). *Munchausen Syndrome by Proxy Abuse: A practical approach.* Butterworth – Heinemann, Oxford.

Eminson D M and Postlethwaite R J (1992) Factitious Illness: recognition and management. *Archives of Disease in Childhood.* **67**: 1510-1516.

Eminson D M and Postlethwaite R J (2000) *Munchausen Syndrome by Proxy Abuse: A practical approach.* Arnold, London.

Falkov A, Mayes K, Diggins M, Silverdale N, and Cox A, (1998) *Crossing Bridges – Training resources for working with mentally ill parents and their children.* Pavilion Publishing, Brighton.

General Medical Council (2006) *Good Medical Practice.* General Medical Council, London.

Gray J and Bentovim A (1996) Illness Induction Syndrome: Paper I – A series of 41 Children from 37 Families Identified at The Great Ormond Street Hospital for Children NHS Trust. *Child Abuse and Neglect.* 20 **8**: 655-673.

Gray J, Bentovim A and Milla P (1995) *The treatment of children and their families where induced illness has been identified.* In: Horwath J and Lawson B (eds) (1995) *Trust Betrayed? Munchausen Syndrome by Proxy – inter-agency child protection and partnership with families.* National Children's Bureau, London.

Griffith J (1988) The Family Systems of Munchausen Syndrome by Proxy. *Family Process.* **27**: 423-437.

HM Government (2006a) *Working Together to Safeguard Children.* London, The Stationary Office. www.everychildmatters.gov.uk/workingtogether

HM Government (2006b) *Information Sharing: Practitioners' guide.* London, Department for Education and Skills.

HM Government (2007) *Statutory guidance on making arrangements to safeguard and promote the welfare of children under section 11 of the Children Act 2004.* London, Department for Education and Skills.

Horwath J and Lawson B (eds) (1995) *Trust Betrayed? Munchausen Syndrome by Proxy: inter-agency child protection and partnership with families*. National Children's Bureau, London.

Human Rights Act 1998 (1998) The Stationery Office, London.

Information Commissioner (2002) *The Use and Disclosure of Health Data*.

Jones D P H (1998) The effectiveness of intervention. In Adcock M and White R (eds) (1998) *Significant Harm: its Management and Outcom*e. pp. 91-119. Significant Publications, Croydon.

Jones D P H and Bools C N (1999) *Factitious illness by proxy*. In David T J (ed) *Recent Advances in Paediatrics*. 17 pp 57-71. Churchill Livingstone, London.

Jones D P H, Byrne G and Newbold C (2002) In Eminson M and Postlethwaite R (2000) *Munchausen Syndrome by Proxy Abuse*: A practical Approach. Butterworth – Heinemann, Oxford.

Jureidini J (1993) Obstetric Factitious Disorder and Munchausen Syndrome by Proxy. *The Journal of Nervous and Mental Disease.* **181** (2): 135-137.

Makar A and Squier P (1990) Munchausen Syndrome by Proxy: father as a perpetrator. *American Journal of Paediatrics.* **85**: 370-373.

Manthei D J, Pierce R L, Rothbaum R J, Manthei U and Keating J P (1988) Munchausen Syndrome by Proxy: Covert Child Abuse. *Journal of Family Violence.* 3 **2**:131-140.

McClure R J, Davis P M, Meadow S R and Sibert J R (1996) Epidemiology of Munchausen syndrome by proxy: non-accidental poisoning and non-accidental suffocation. *Archives of Disease in Childhood.* **75**: 57-61.

McGuire T L and Feldman K W (1998) Psychological morbidity of children subjected to Munchausen Syndrome by Proxy. *Paediatrics* **83**: 289-292.

Neale B, Bools C and Meadow R (1991) Problems in the assessment and management of Munchausen Syndrome by proxy abuse. *Children and Society.* 5 **4**: 324-333.

Nicol A R and Eccles M (1985) Psychotherapy for Munchausen Syndrome by Proxy. *Archives of Diseases in Childhood.* **60**: 344-348.

Nursing and Midwifery Council (2006) *Advice on Record Keeping*. NMC, London.

Regulation of Investigatory Powers Act 2000 (2000) HMSO, London.

Rogers D, Tripp J, Bentovim A, Robinson A, Berry D and Golding R (1976) Non-accidental poisoning: an extended syndrome of child abuse. *British Medical Journal.* **1**: 793-796.

Rosenberg D (1987) Web of Deceit: A literature review of Munchausen Syndrome by Proxy. *Child Abuse and Neglect.* **11**:547-563.

Royal College of Paediatrics and Child Health (2002) *Fabricated or Induced Illness by Carers*. RCPCH, London.

Samuels M, McClaughlin W, Jacobson R, Poets C and Southall D (1992) Fourteen cases of imposed upper airway obstruction. *Archives of Disease in Childhood.* **67**: 162-170.

Sanders M J (1995) Symptom coaching: Factitious disorders by proxy with older children. Special Issue: The impact of the family on child adjustment and psychopathology. *Clinical Psychology Review*. **15**: 423-442.

Schreier H A and Libow J A (1993) Hurting for Love: Munchausen by Proxy Syndrome. The Guilford Press, New York.